Blazing the
Old Cattle Trail

Blazing the Old Cattle Trail

Grant MacEwan

FIFTH
HOUSE
PUBLISHERS

Front cover photograph of Bert Kitchen, Alberta, performing the "wedding ring" with his lariat, late 1920s, courtesy Pat Humphreys (daughter).
Cover and interior design by The Studio Group.

The publisher gratefully acknowledges the support of The Canada Council for the Arts and the Department of Canadian Heritage.

We acknowledge the financial support of the Government of Canada through the Book Publishing Industry Development Program for our publishing activities.

Printed in Canada.
00 01 02 03 04 / 5 4 3 2 1

Canadian Cataloguing in Publication Data
MacEwan, Grant, 1902-2000.
   Blazing the old cattle trail

   ISBN 1-894004-63-9

   1. Cattle drives--Prairie Provinces--History. I. Title.
FC3209.C37M33 2000   971.2   C00-910910-2
F1060.M1328 2000

Fifth House Ltd.
A Fitzhenry & Whiteside Company
1511–1800 4 St. SW
Calgary, Alberta, Canada
T2S 2S5

Grant MacEwan, 1986

About the Author

GRANT MACEWAN was born in Brandon, Manitoba on August 12, 1902. Educated in Brandon, and Melfort, Saskatchewan, he went on to graduate from Ontario Agricultural College in 1926 and Iowa State College in 1928. He was a professor of animal husbandry at the University of Saskatchewan and department head from 1928 to 1946, and Dean of Agriculture at the University of Manitoba from 1946 to 1951.

He began his political career in 1951, when he stood as the Liberal candidate in Brandon's federal by-election. He moved to Calgary soon after his defeat and served as an elected alderman from 1953 to 1959. Elected as an MLA in 1955, he was leader of the Alberta Liberal Party from 1958 to 1960. He was elected mayor of Calgary in 1963 and served in this capacity until 1966.

Grant MacEwan served as lieutenant-governor of Alberta from 1965 to 1974 and was made a member of the Order of Canada in 1975. Grant MacEwan Community College in Edmonton was named in his honour.

After 1963, he published four agricultural texts and some 50 books on historical subjects, averaging close to a book each year between 1970 and 1990. His latest book, *Watershed: Reflections by Grant MacEwan*, is being published in September 2000 by NeWest Press.

Grant MacEwan's wide-ranging experiences in academic, political, and literary circles often put him in the public eye. He won the hearts of thousands of people across the prairies with his engaging personality, accessibility, and the hundreds of entertaining stories he had at his fingertips. He died on June 15, 2000.

Contents

Preface

GRANT MACEWAN'S ENORMOUS REPUTATION as a writer, politician, conservationist, and public figure sometimes obscures the fact that he was first and foremost an agriculturalist specializing in animal husbandry. His practical background with cattle is particularly impressive, and he was involved in several pioneering cattle-feeding experiments while at the University of Saskatchewan. He was also a prominent cattle judge.

Blazing the Old Cattle Trail is infused with MacEwan's knowledge of the Western Canadian cattle industry and the individuals who dominated it. There are sketches on sheep, pigs, and horses, and some references to the Red River experience in the early 19th century, but MacEwan concentrates mainly on the colourful cattle drives characteristic of the Western Canadian open range ranching era of 1875-1906. By using these drives as a focus for wider discussion and observations, MacEwan tells us about the romance, hardships, heroism, and humour of the West, and brings alive a period that, for most Canadians, embodies most graphically the frontier spirit.

MacEwan ranges far and wide in this collection. Some accounts are solidly based in the history of the cattle industry. The movement of cattle from the United States to stock the Canadian range in the later 1870s and early 1880s is documented through the Emerson & Lynch and Cochrane cattle drives. The saga of moving cattle to the Yukon gold fields is also well covered. On the other hand, his stories of sheep and pig drives, or the thrilling account of the illegal movement of a bunch of thoroughbred horses from Calgary to Montana tell us as much or more about the human spirit than about events of historical significance.

An important component of *Blazing the Old Cattle Trail* lies in the numerous character sketches that appear almost incidentally in the narrative. Prominent, though hardly well-known, figures such as the early cattle industry's Tom Lynch, Frank White, Billy Henry, and Tony Day receive solid treatment. Always interested in the individual and a good story, MacEwan blends the two in this popular account of cattle drives in the early Canadian West.

Max Foran
Western Heritage Centre
Cochrane, Alberta
June 28, 2000

Trail Dust In Other Lands

EVER SINCE THE PATRIARCH, ABRAHAM, "very rich in cattle," drove westward from Ur of the Chaldees to find pasture in the Land of Canaan, stockmen have been driving trail herds to far places and performing some of the most amazing and daring feats in the world of agriculture. Cattle trails, it seems, cross the pages of history at all stages of civilization.

Abraham, like innumerable cattlemen since his time, was attracted by the frontier ranges. Presumably, neighbors were becoming too numerous where he ran cattle in the Valley of the Euphrates, and he wanted the freedom and expansiveness of country to the west. But there were many reasons for history's long drives attended by dangers in a score of shapes.

Often the trail offered the only means of taking meat animals to a market but sometimes it was a matter of making annual pilgrimages to distant grazing grounds, or introducing breeding stock to new country. Nor should it be overlooked that many of the stirring drives of the centuries were directed by skillful rustlers who sought to move stolen cattle or sheep the greatest possible distance in the shortest possible space of time. If the thieves could drive their ill-gotten gain across one or more boundaries, so much the better. English rustlers being forced to make hurried tracks northward toward hide-away glens in the Scottish Highlands offer the most familiar example but it should be noted that the

MacEwans and Grants were not the only free enterprisers indulging in that trade.

Most countries knew something about long annual journeys with livestock, to utilize the grazing in remote and rough territories. Such was the case in Spain where southern sheepmen took their flocks northward a few hundred miles each summer to graze on inter-mountain grass. And now and then, Spanish flocks were taken still farther northward to cross the Pyrenees and be smuggled into France. Probably the French breed known as Rambouillet owes its origin to Spanish Merinos that patient and reckless herders chased over the mountains in defiance of border restrictions.

⤙━◆━O━◆━━⤚

IN A CONTINENT-WIDE COUNTRY like the United States, a certain amount of trailing was inevitable. Illinois cattle were driven for slaughter at Boston—1200 miles—in 1840 and what was more thoroughly publicized, literally millions of Texas cattle were herded northward to furnish seed-stock for the new ranges of Wyoming and Montana and neighboring states.

That cattle-moving program out of Texas was the most gigantic in history. Most people have heard something of the huge herds which were trailed far beyond their natural horizons in the years after the Civil War. It is fortunate that the Texas tales about bad-tempered cattle with horns as long as buffalo-guns have been recorded and one can forgive a Texan's understandable inclination to boast about the drives.

Naturally, the great herds of semi-domesticated, unclaimed longhorns occupying the southern grass would attract those rugged fellows with an affinity for stock saddles. The long-legged, long-horned, narrow-backed, horse-faced animals were Spanish in origin but their dispositions had deteriorated since ancestors arrived with the colonists who followed Columbus to the New World. They hated the sight of human forms and were inclined to hit for the rimrock when they spotted them.

A strong point about the longhorns was their prolificacy. Since they multiplied faster than local markets for beef, the Commonwealth of Texas became overrun with them. In 1860 there were three and one-half million cattle in Texas and, for the most part, they were not worth the time and trouble it took to catch and brand them.

A few herds were cut out and driven north before the Civil War but these were more or less experimental and it wasn't until 1866 that trailing became a bustling business. Two hundred and sixty thousand head were driven out of Texas that year, most of them being directed to Sadalia, Missouri, and Baxter Springs, Kansas, at which points they could be loaded on freight cars and shipped to St. Louis.

In the following year, trail's end shifted to Abilene, Kansas, largely through the enterprise of the two McCoy brothers from Springfield, Illinois. Sensing the need for better terminal facilities, the two young fellows fixed upon this little Kansas village, with plenty of grass and water nearby, as the best place for the trail to connect with the new Kansas Pacific Railway. Workmen began about the first of July and two months later the promoters could point to a shipping centre with stockyard accommodation for 3000 cattle, weighing facilities and three-storey hotel destined to witness some of the most fabulous cowboy celebrations in range history.

Before the new yarding accommodation was completed, riders were intercepting the cattlemen as they made their slow way northward, inviting them to make Abilene the trail's end. Men of the dusty and dangerous trail were glad to accept and, almost overnight, like a man who wins an Irish sweepstake, Abilene sprang into prominence. At once, the residents of what had been an unprepossessing shack-town found their community over-run with rip-roaring cowboys, gamblers, gunmen—even women.

The famous cowtown continued to be the northern terminus of the busiest cattle trail in the world for about five years. Then the trade shifted to Wichita and Ellsworth, Kansas, and in 1876, Dodge City won the cattlemen's preference and began a gigantic business.

According to federal estimates, not less than seven million southern cattle were driven across the states of Texas and Oklahoma to Dodge City between 1873 and 1887. It was like a mighty river of cattle, seemingly inexhaustible.

>─┤◆├─◯─┤◆├─◄

BUT REGARDLESS OF THE GEOGRAPHIC LOCATION of Trail's End, driving Texas cattle was a job for courageous men only. Attendants knew that the nervous and spooky longhorns were easily alarmed and would stampede at the slightest provocation. After a stampede, especially at night, there would be some broken legs as well as broken horns and, indeed, some cattle would never be recovered. Attendants knew, also, that Indians watched for opportunities to attack. Their motive might be revenge or gain—or both. It was a favorite trick with some prairie tribes to scare the herd into a stampede, then hire themselves to the herd owner to help gather the scattered cattle. There was the added incentive that some cattle were never gathered after a stampede dispersion, and the Indians would get these at some later time and feast upon fresh beef.

And when cattle increased in value, whites as well as Indians would steal a steer or a thousand steers if there seemed a reasonable chance of escaping the bloody consequences.

Hence the men who rode with the trail herds both north and south of the Canada-United States boundary had to be alert to all possible dangers, had to be hardy and ready to shoot it out with anybody—Indian or white—who threatened to interfere. They were not the guitar-playing dudes but, rather, hard-riding fellows who accepted searing heat, cold rain and the necessity of sleeping in damp bedrolls with no more hesitation than they accepted an increase in pay or a Saturday night in town.

From the Texas range to Abilene or Dodge City took two or three months. There was no advantage in loitering, and no profit in hurrying beyond what the cattle could do comfortably or without loss of weight. Twelve to fifteen miles per day was fast enough if shrinkage and loss of condition were to be avoided.

Barring accidents or trouble, there was a certain fairly standard pattern about a day on the trail. For the first two hours of early morning, the cattle were allowed to graze as they moved slowly in the proper direction. That was followed by a more brisk movement until noon when there would be a rest period of two or three hours. After that mid-day rest, there was more grazing as the animals were driven slowly for several hours before being allowed to settle for the night.

And, oh the nights! Somebody had to be on duty throughout and nobody fancied the assignment. It was lonely and the night hours seemed like weeks. Everything was magnified. The squeak of a mouse could sound loud enough to be fearsome. And anybody with a superstitious turn of mind was sure to see ghostly figures flitting through the shadows.

Two thousand or two thousand five hundred head made an average herd for the long trail leading out of Texas but some men undertook to drive bigger ones. There is record of a drive consisting of twenty-five thousand cattle being inched northward and ultimately arriving at its destination. Instead of being driven in the usual way and at usual pace, however, that big herd was merely guided and allowed to travel at a speed of the animals' own choosing. Progress wouldn't exceed four or five miles a day but in a hundred days that could mean four hundred or five hundred miles. Anyway, the cattle were delivered.

In being driven northward, those famous herds were projected toward Canada and some did reach Canadian grass. But Canadians had their first experiences in long distance driving long before the Texas cattle were moving.

Drives to, from and on Canadian soil? There were lots of them and some must rank among the most notable in history. The tragedy is that Canadians didn't take better care of their stories about those trailing exploits involving courage, patience and endurance. Only in being more widely and loudly publicized did the Texas drives surpass many of those with which Canadians should be familiar.

Adam and Eve of
the Cattle Kingdom

>─┤─◀▸──O──◀▸─┤─◁

ADAM AND EVE WERE THE FIRST CATTLE in the Selkirk Settlement
at Red River and, of course, the colonists hoped fervently that
they'd be "fruitful and multiply and replenish" the new soil with
oxen and milk cows. With three other cattle specimens they may
share the distinction of being the first of their race in all the area
now marked by four western provinces. Understandably, they
were not delivered at the remote point where Winnipeg stands
today without great effort and ingenuity.

There is reason to believe that the beginning of the 19th century—a dozen years before the Selkirk colonists arrived—found the
present agricultural section of the West a complete vacuum as far as
domestic cattle, sheep and pigs were concerned. Beyond the area,
Albany Fort may have had a few cattle, sheep and goats surviving
from early importations and Moose Factory Journal reported the
slaughter of two cows and three pigs on March 24, 1783. But those
posts were on James Bay and far from the present-day farm belt
where Indian dogs of many colors and, horses held uneasily by
horse-stealing tribesmen were the only domestic animals.

In bringing the initial foundations of domestic livestock to
the new land, animals could be driven overland or carried in
canoes. There was no other way. But one thing was certain: a
farming community without cattle and other livestock was

unthinkable, especially to settlers with British ideals concerning agriculture. Cattle had to come.

>—I—◆≻—O—◅≻—I—◁

THE FIRST OF THE SELKIRK PEOPLE, under the leadership of Highlander Miles Macdonell, sailed away from Stornoway, Scotland, in July, 1811, leaving behind on the quay eight young cattle provided by Lord Selkirk. The obstacle to taking the cattle was the necessity of carrying enough fresh water for the long voyage—one which took sixty-one days.

Macdonell and his advance guard wintered on the cold and inhospitable shores of Hudson Bay and in the spring of 1812, the twenty-two courageous trailblazers started up the Hayes River in their long and shallow canoes, knowing their destination beside the Red River to be some seven hundred land and water miles—including thirty-six portages or carrying places—to the south.

Macdonell had been warned: this was a tricky route with confusing water courses, formidable waterfalls, deep lakes, shallow water with the character of swamps and many miles of fast current demanding the use of tracking lines. But after about two weeks of paddling on rivers and lakes, Macdonell and his men came to Oxford House, a small Hudson's Bay Company trading post encompassed by a sturdy stockade made from upright pine logs with tops sharpened like pencil-points. On a grassy hill rising from the shore of Oxford Lake, the setting was a pretty one where about the only noises ever heard were those made by wind or wolves.

The men were still less than half way to Red River but they stopped to relax and there, to their very great surprise, were two young cattle, a bull and yearling heifer, contradicting their belief that no cattle existed in all of Rupert's Land. Evidently the animals had been brought from the Old Country as calves in the previous year. But where they came from mattered little; the Selkirk men, with the practical minds of Highlanders, were thinking more about the animals' destiny than their origin. Why let these young cows be wasted at a northern trading post when they could serve a most essential purpose in the new farming venture?

The men resolved to take the two cattle along to Red River and the Hudson's Bay Company trader surrendered wisely to the combined determination of twenty-two resolute Scots and Irishmen. The two young cattle—christened Adam and Eve— may have remembered calfhood experiences in boats. Anyway, they accepted the necessity of travelling again and two canoes with a yearling critter in each rode lower than usual in the water. Nobody could overlook the increased danger of upsetting if a bull in a canoe became obstreperous, especially in fast or tricky water.

Fortunately, Adam and Eve, on their best bovine behavior, learned to step into and out of their boats with exercised care and they grazed quietly when men were carrying bales and boats over the numerous portages. No hay was taken from Oxford House and stops—at least two a day—to allow the animals to forage, became routine. Finding satisfactory grazing and suitable places for loading and unloading demanded almost constant attention.

After leaving Oxford House there was the deep water of what the voyageurs called Holey lake, then a sluggish, grassy section of river and more portages. At Hill Gate, rocky and picturesque cliffs rose sixty or eighty feet to wall the stream for three-quarters of a mile, and at what was called Painted Stone Portage, travellers saw a long, low rock which divided marshy waters flowing respectively to the Hayes and Nelson rivers. Indians with spooky superstitions painted the stone and deposited gifts for members of the spirit world in the surrounding water. Such gifts dropped beside the big stone were like premiums on Indian life insurance.

Less than a week after leaving Oxford House, the Selkirk men passed Jack River House on Playgreen lake and knew that the laborious experiences of portaging were nearly all behind them. The next stop was at the top of Lake Winnipeg and then there was the long stretch of generally still water, terminating at the marshy mouth of the Red River. On August 30, exactly fifty-five days after leaving Hudson Bay, Miles Macdonell and his advance guard camped on the banks of the Red River, where Winnipeg stands today. In its primitive state it was no Garden of Eden but, nevertheless, Adam and Eve must have found the grazing far superior to anything they had seen at far-away Oxford House. There, in their new surroundings, they were to bring practical comfort to the settlers arriving a few weeks later.

>-◆>-O-<◆>-<

THE FOLLOWING WINTER was a hard one for both settlers and cattle. It was long, and famine was a constant threat. But in the spring of 1813, Peter Fidler, faithful and prolific servant of the Hudson's Bay Company, learned about three other cattle in Rupert's Land, a cow, a bull and a heifer owned by the rival North-West Company at its post on the Assiniboine. Presumably, the cow and bull had been brought as calves from Montreal and the heifer was born in the west country. Anyway, nobody needed such stock as much as the new settlers beside the Red River, and Fidler journeyed up the Assiniboine and succeeded in buying the three head for one hundred pounds.

By this time, Eve had a calf and the Selkirk Settlers could count a total of six cattle. These western provinces, which today have around five million cattle, may have had exactly six head in that spring of 1813.

But cattle raising was never without disappointments. The bull bought from the North-West Company became vicious and had to be slaughtered in the fall of 1813. That in itself was not serious because the masculine Adam remained to fulfill all duties as head of the herd and bull beef could be used most acceptably by the settlers. But with the approach of spring, Adam yielded to a temptation to wander. Straying from the home corral was a sin common to bulls and before Adam had time to repent, he was completely lost in the woods south of the settlement.

A search was organized but all efforts to locate the delin-quent bull failed. Worried settlers hoped the wayward fellow would wander back in his own good time as he had wandered away, but Adam didn't come back. Nothing was seen of him until break-up on the river when the still-frozen body of a bloated bull was observed floating down the Red on a big cake of ice.

Now the only herd of cattle in Rupert's Land had no bull, and the cattle outlook was bleak indeed. Not until after the bloody Battle of Seven Oaks on soil which is now in the city of Winnipeg were cattle numbers augmented. Lord Selkirk's pri-vate army on its way from the East to the relief of the oppressed colonists, seized the Rainy Lake Post, property of the hated North-West Company. At that fort, situated in what is now Western Ontario, the soldiers found three oxen, three cows and a young bull. Here were prizes of war, too good to be left behind—almost too good to be true—and plans were made to drive or lead the animals to the Red River.

It was winter. Two of the oxen were shod so that they might assist the five horses already in the party to haul the sleighs. The third ox, unshod, promptly slipped on ice and so injured himself that it was thought wise to slaughter him and salvage the meat. When additional work stock was needed on the trail, the young bull was hitched and even the cows were drafted to do a share in pulling the loaded sleighs.

Finally, the rescue force arrived at Fort Douglas beside the Red River where, according to Professor A. S. Morton, "The bull and cows, discharged from the army, were now like Adam and Eve of five years back, to multiply and help build a farm-ing community."

⤖◆◦◆⤚

BUT RED RIVER COLONY seemed a hard country to those pio-neers who were planting the seeds of an agricultural industry. The bushel and one-half of seed wheat carried by Macdonell's men and planted beside the river proved unsuitable and the crop did not mature. Wheat planted in 1814 was lost to frost, and local warfare between settlers and the Nor'-Westers prevented the harvesting of crops in the next two years. In 1817 it was frost which again destroyed the chance of harvest and then there were two years of grasshopper attack. It would have been easy to conclude that further attempts to till the unfriendly soil were futile.

And success with cattle was proving no better than with wheat. Before a year elapsed, the Rainy Lake bull was dead and some of the other cattle had been killed and eaten by hungry Indians. When Lord Selkirk visited his colony in 1817, he was visibly disappointed at the absence of progress. There was extremely little to show for those first trying years of farming. Only the big annual harvest of buffalo meat, dried for winter use or blended with crushed saskatoon berries and melted fat to make pemmican, saved the settlers from starvation.

But with Scottish and Irish ideas about good farming practice, the settlers lost none of their longing to have livestock. Cattle could and would mean milk, butter, cheese, meat, draught power and security. Lord Selkirk agreed and admitted that he had already enquired about the possibility of driving a really worthwhile herd from the East or South. He would provide the money for fifty heifers, he said, and a thousand dollars for the expense of bringing them in. It was a prospect appearing almost as attractive to Scottish settlers as Selkirk's promise to send them a Presbyterian minister.

But where within driving distance could such a herd be bought? To drive from Montreal would be nigh impossible. Driving from the South might be easier but nobody was sure the cattle were available there. And where was there a man who cared so little for his own comfort and safety that he would accept the task of finding and delivering a herd—perhaps driving it half way across the continent?

As for the good cow, Eve, there is reason to believe she was still alive when Selkirk made his visit—also one or two of her offspring—and it may be possible that progeny, far removed, are even today scattered across the farming country.

The Dousman Drives

IT WAS SMALL WONDER that Lord Selkirk found the Red River Settlement in gloom when he visited there in 1817. For five years, little but failure attended the settlers' efforts to produce wheat, acquire cattle and become self sufficient. Even the twenty-one Spanish Merino sheep brought with settlers arriving late in 1812 had disappeared, having been victims of coyotes, Indians and poor management.

Selkirk's proposal to import a sizeable herd of breeding cattle from Baldoon in Upper Canada or somewhere far south was both welcome and comforting, but an undertaking of such magnitude could not be concluded at once. Appreciating immediate needs, the sympathetic and resourceful Earl advised that steps be taken to domesticate prairie buffalo and cross them with domestic cattle. Evidently the settlers did capture some of the wild young things but there is nothing to show that hybridization was successful.

In negotiating arrangements for the purchase and delivery of that long-anticipated herd of cattle with which to stock Red River farms, delays might well have been expected. Selkirk died in April, 1820, and thus did not see the culmination of his bold and worthy plan. Before his death, however, he completed the initial negotiations. With the aid of Colonel Robert Dickson, lady's man and firebrand who had been trading in furs in the

Mississippi Valley, Selkirk met with a robust fellow who was ready for the task of moving cattle, a thousand miles or more if necessary. His name was Dousman—Michael Dousman—and in the light of subsequent events, nobody earned more fully a place of honor in the hall of distinguished cattlemen than did this man.

Dousman also had indulged in trading south of the border and was familiar with the trails and dangers of the Interior. He knew all the tributaries of the Mississippi and understood the hazards in crossing them. He understood the Indian character. It is doubtful, however, if he had any early experience with cattle.

One can do no more than speculate about the man's appearance but it is not difficult to picture him as a long, lean specimen with sharp features, untrimmed black hair and legs bowed slightly from long days astride a buffalo-hunting cayuse. A two-fisted fellow, vigorous and self-reliant, Dousman could ride, hunt, run and paddle with the best of them.

><+>•○•<+><

NOBODY AT RED RIVER knew how far a man would have to go for cattle, although Lord Selkirk, after leaving Red River in 1817, travelled far south and looked at herds in Missouri and Kentucky. Evidently the farther south a person went at that time, the better the chance of locating available cattle. Dousman may have known that far south on the plains of Texas there were growing numbers of unclaimed Spanish cattle with long horns and bad tempers. Certainly he knew there were hungry and ruthless Indians and other dangers lurking in the intervening hundreds of miles.

Anyway, by the terms of a contract signed in June, 1819, Dousman was to secure seventy-six cows, twenty oxen, four bulls, six mares and a stallion. These he would be required to deliver at Big Stone Lake, roughly four hundred miles straight south of the present "Gateway to the West," the site of Winnipeg, or drive right through to the settlement. But Dousman had no misgivings; he was more familiar with the

Mississippi valley where he had dodged tomahawk-wielding natives and traded and hunted, than the settlers were with their own valley of the Red River.

He explained to the Selkirk people where they would meet him in early autumn, at a point south of Big Stone Lake, and was on his way.

What kind of cattle would Dousman find in the country beyond St. Louis at that time? What would be their color and type? Foundation stock in that part of the State of Missouri might have come from the Atlantic states where British breeds predominated, or from Texas where cattle of Spanish origin were increasing in numbers and wildness. Texas would have been more accessible and, if a person be permitted to speculate, the cattle Dousman rounded up in the St. Louis countryside were probably long in the horns, long in legs and extremely short of the kind of disposition so much desired in a family cow. Their conformation would be rough and inferior but they would be about as hardy as mustang horses, and good travellers.

Dousman must have started northward about midsummer—actually too late, considering the twelve hundred or fifteen hundred miles to Fort Douglas beside the Red River. Progress on the trail was all that might be expected but for reasons unknown, the Selkirk colony men failed to meet him at the United States point as planned. The settlers should have had some knowledge of that section because just a year earlier, after two years of crop failure caused by grasshoppers, men from Red River went on snowshoes as far as Prairie du Chien where they bought two hundred and fifty bushels of seed wheat and rafted it back to the settlement when the rivers were high in the spring.

While Dousman waited, cold weather set in. As long as the ground was bare, prairie grazing was unlimited but when snow fell, the cattle, feeding only on the grasses and other plants protruding above the snow cover, suffered immediately from hunger. As winter advanced, cattle died and in the spring there remained only nineteen head from the original herd of nearly two hundred.

At some later date, the few surviving cattle were driven on to the settlement north of the boundary and, no doubt, they brought at least slight relief. But Dousman turned again to the south, saying to his helpers: "We'll try it again; we'll start earlier and we'll have better luck."

And so, in the spring of 1821, the hardy plainsman had another herd—two hundred of the unco-operative cattle—and was on the trail earlier in the season. Making a good twelve miles a day, he swam a lot of rivers for the second time, passed Prairie du Chien in July and was congratulating himself on the prospect of having the herd at Fort Douglas before the end of September. But, after travelling eight hundred trail miles and getting close to Big Stone Lake—about the centre of the Sioux country—Dousman heard the fiendish whoops of mounted men, riding hard toward him. The meaning was unmistakable—Indians, the most belligerent tribesmen on the plains. The northern Sioux hadn't seen domestic cattle very often but knew what they were and that they were good to eat.

While the painted warriors ignored completely the accompanying white men, arrows flew and cattle fell.

Dousman, with unrestrained anger, protested. But what was the use? What could be gained by obstructing? Hopelessly outnumbered, he knew he'd be lucky if he escaped without an arrow in his own temple.

Terrified cattle stampeded in various directions, and Indians pursued in the manner of a buffalo hunt. When the ferocious Sioux attacked a buffalo herd of moderate size, they commonly aimed to kill everything in it and a herd of domestic cattle didn't seem to warrant any different treatment. As Indians, delighted with unexpected good fortune, swooped close to running cows, shot and repeated, Dousman saw his cattle dropping, one after another. When the noise ended and dust subsided, there wasn't a single cow, bull or calf standing. Most of the cattle were dead; others, wounded, writhed in agony. Avariciously, the natives fell to the task of removing tongues and other favorite portions from hot carcasses. Dousman could do nothing but watch.

Either the Indians were hungry or they merely craved a change of meat. In any case, Dousman, four hundred trail miles from Fort Douglas and eight hundred from his starting point, was completely out of cattle. For the second successive year, the long drive ended in failure.

Accepting the dictates of cruel fate, he turned his saddle and pack horses and with no reason to hurry, slowly retraced his way southward. At least, he'd be back among friends beside the Mississippi before the winter weather set in.

>–I–◆–O–◆–I–<

HAD THE SETTLERS AT RED RIVER known of Dousman's second misfortune, there would have been added reason for gloom. But others with the wild spirit of frontier adventure recognized opportunity for gain and, as it happened, a comparatively small herd from Prairie du Chien beside the big river, was on the trail at the same time. Joseph Rolette was the promoter and Alexis Bailly, the man in charge—both French Canadians who had taken to trading along the Mississippi.

Luck rode with Bailly; he missed the Sioux or the Sioux missed him and some time in September or October, he reached the Selkirk Settlement, completing an eight hundred mile drive. He readily sold the cows and oxen at prices which made the undertaking profitable. As a result of this effort and the few cattle salvaged from Dousman's first drive, the cattle population at Red River in 1822—ten years after the colony was started—stood at three bulls, six oxen, forty-five cows and thirty-nine calves. But such numbers were still far from being adequate, far from permitting even one cow per family. Human population had increased and the need for more cattle had scarcely lessened.

As for Dousman, one would naturally expect him to abandon the contract to deliver a big herd. Most men would have had enough. But he was not one to give up and after spring weather came in 1823, he was once again driving cattle over the trail northward from St. Louis. The character of the route was unchanged but Dousman and his horse knew it better, knew where to find the water holes and the best river crossings. With good fortune, he drove through the Sioux country without being detected and on August 28, he completed what was probably the most notable cattle drive on the North American continent, delivering one hundred and seventy cattle at the new settlement.

Settlers were overjoyed and Dousman was rewarded. Cattle that were surplus to the contract he had made long before with Lord Selkirk were now offered for sale privately and settlers bought them eagerly, paying ten or twelve pounds per head for cows and fifteen pounds or more for oxen.

>-+-+>-+-O-+-<+-+-<

REV. JOHN WEST of the Anglican Church, returning to Red River in October, 1822, a few weeks after Dousman delivered the cattle, learned about the season's good harvest and saw stacks of feed. Best of all, he saw the "more than one hundred and fifty head of cattle" which had just arrived and concluded that it marked the dawn of a new and better day for the settlers. At once he bought two of the cows for the mission school and admitted relief "from anxiety as to provisions for the children."

Two years later, in 1824, another big southern herd was driven to the Selkirk Settlement, leading Red River historian, Alexander Ross, to write, "How cheering it was to behold the numerous small herds of domestic cattle that enliven the plains so lately swarming with wild buffalo, only those can say who, like the writer, have watched the savage aspect of things daily, hourly, yielding to the more genial fruits of civilization."

And Michael Dousman? He didn't stay around to be honored for his part in bringing a better standard of living and more security to the first farmers in the West but, nevertheless, he was the hero and deserved to be remembered.

Sheep for the Settlement

SELKIRK SETTLERS, WITH SPINNING WHEELS, wanted and needed sheep. As those first western farmers knew very well, sheep would be the means of providing homemade woollen clothing as well as meat. Many of the newcomers, former Scottish crofters with heather in their shepherds' beards, knew more about sheep than about other livestock and considered them of chief importance to their future in the new and untested world.

The bull and heifer brought from Oxford House by Miles Macdonell and his advance guard in 1812, were the first farm animals to which the immigrants could lay claim but when the next group arrived a few weeks later, they had with them twenty-one aristocratic Merina sheep.

Lord Selkirk's reasoning was good and logical. Wool, in addition to being the raw material for homespun, might become an important commodity for export. Farmers must have something to sell. The good Earl had a vision of Red River wool being packed in tight bales and moved by York boats or freight canoes to Hudson Bay, thence by sailing ships to the woollen mills of England. It was a nice dream and to give it the best chance of a successful fulfillment, the Red River flocks would have to be started with selected breeding stock. The Merino breed, with its reputation for unsurpassed quality of wool, was Lord Selkirk's choice. Rejecting the lowly

Blackface sheep of Scotland, he sent to Spain for the choice little flock which ultimately reached Red River with the settlers in 1812.

The animals made the trip from Hudson Bay by canoe, just like the Bible-carrying settlers themselves. There were the inevitable portages and obstacles on the seven hundred mile route, and having sheep to feed and care for added to the troubles.

The Merinos made the trip well enough but their reception at the forks of the Assiniboine and Red rivers was mixed indeed. To Prairie Indians the new animals appeared strange and more or less terrible. Encountering animals with unknown habits and appetites might well cause worry. Who among the uninformed could be sure these creatures were not man-eaters? Some of the less brave of the braves were seen seeking safety in the higher branches of trees while the inoffensive Merinos grazed peacefully below.

But everything seemed to work against the sheep. Coyotes, Indians and Indian dogs were soon to discover the distinctive palatability of mutton. Then there was cold weather when the surviving ewes were lambing. Instead of increasing, the sheep were decreasing—down to nine ewes, four lambs and two rams in 1814.

In this isolated community where nearly every wife took pride in her spinning skill, insufficient wool was almost as serious as being short of salt.

>-<>-O-<>-<

THE HUDSON'S BAY COMPANY was still hopeful about sheep becoming a good line of production for Red River and another flock was imported to York Factory in 1821. While awaiting freight canoes to transport them to the settlement, the animals were held in temporary pens on an island in the Hayes River. There misfortune overtook them; the river rose several feet and most of the sheep, including all the rams, were drowned. Nicholas Garry, writing from York Factory on September 6, 1821, notes, "The remainder of the colonists embarked today in five large boats for the Red

River and one small boat which contained a few passengers with the remainder of the sheep which were saved from drowning."

At this point, with sheep being plagued constantly by misfortune, Settler John Pritchard had an inspiration: why not forget about sheep and go for buffalo wool? Thousands of buffalo were being killed annually, he pointed out, and it would be a simple matter to clip the so-called wool from the hides and export it for spinning. It sounded like a good idea and Pritchard's enthusiasm led in 1821 to the formation of the Buffalo Wool Company. It would only be a matter of time, it seemed, until every person who subscribed capital would be receiving handsome dividends.

The coats of slaughtered buffalo were indeed sheared and the product exported but one thing Pritchard overlooked: the buffalo fibres are hairs and not wool. In passing through the English mills, the long guard hairs made technical and mechanical troubles and the English millers wanted no more "buffalo wool." Pritchard's company went bankrupt and, again, public interest turned to sheep.

>—◄►—○—◄►—◄

WHAT FOLLOWED WAS THE MOST AMBITIOUS SHEEP scheme of all, patterned on Michael Dousman's cattle drive from St. Louis, Missouri. Company Governor George Simpson, anxious to see the settlers producing something for sale abroad, gave his support. He had encouraged the Buffalo Wool Company and when it failed, imported flax and hemp seed, hopeful that these crops would provide weaving material. Now he was ready to co-operate in any possible way to advance the plan to deliver a band of southern sheep.

The man named to head the buying and driving expedition was William Glen Rae, clerk in the Hudson's Bay Company service, and with him were associated nine others, including J. B. Bourke, a retired company clerk who carried scars from the bloody Battle of Seven Oaks, and Robert Campbell who grew up on a Perthshire sheep farm and whose unpublished journal holds the best account of the adventure.

Campbell was working as an assistant manager at the Experimental Farm beside the Assiniboine, four miles west of the mouth, when told to hold himself in readiness for the long journey. The party of ten, with two carts and eight saddle horses, started south on November 8, 1832. As far as Pembina there was a trail; after that it was a case of following the river and hoping to avoid a meeting with Sioux Indians. While in that area over which these, the most truculant of prairie tribesmen, roamed, the men from Red River wasted no time. At three A.M., they took to the trail; at eight or nine A.M., they stopped for breakfast, if wood and water were available; at sundown they stopped for supper but always moved again for a distance of two or three miles before making night camp, just in case the curls of smoke from the supper-time camp fires might attract the attention of roving Natives.

Indeed, the fears inspiring such precautions were not unfounded. Later, the men learned that a war party of Sioux did follow their trail, giving up after three days of unsuccessful pursuit.

The travellers had hoped to be at St. Peter's Post on the Mississippi, opposite Fort Snelling, in time to get a boat to St. Louis. But arriving on December 1, they learned that the last boat had gone. Actually, the river was beginning to freeze and there was snow on the ground. After some days of travel by sleigh, the river appeared to be navigable again and the men took to canoes, only to find at a point south of Prairie du Chien that ice was forming again. Having left their horses behind, they now had no choice but to continue on foot. They crossed the Illinois River at Bairdstown, continued on through Jacksonville and saw St. Louis on January 3, 1833, eight weeks and an estimated one thousand five hundred miles or more from home.

>─◄►─○─◄►─◄

FOR THE NEXT SIX WEEKS the men from the North travelled out from St. Louis and St. Charles, looking for sheep. Sure enough they found sheep but either they were not for sale or the prices were too high for the parsimonious Mr. Rae.

"You'll do better in Kentucky," was the advice and, moving on eastward, the men made a deal at Versailles for one thousand one hundred sheep and lambs. The seller agreed to shear early so the sheep would travel more easily and on May 2, all was in readiness for the long drive from Kentucky to Red River. In the first few days on the trail—difficult days as anybody knowing sheep would understand—two hundred and seventy more sheep and lambs were added to the band, making a total of one thousand three hundred and seventy head.

Sheep are never overly co-operative but on May 15, Campbell wrote that they were moving along very well, "ten or twelve miles a day." Ahead, however, was more trouble than anybody suspected. There were rivers to cross. There were flies and sore feet. And after passing Peoria, sheep and shepherds faced the most trying tests of all—spear grass, rattlesnakes and maggots. What could be worse?

In one day, five sheep were killed by rattlesnakes and over a few weeks the losses ran to hundreds due to the barbed seeds from maturing speargrass. After crossing the Mississippi at Rock Island, Rae called for a halt to shear the sheep for the second time in less than two months, thinking that short wool would be less likely to pick up the treacherous grass spears. It was a sickening experience with millions of maggots infesting the wounds and irritations created by the inescapable seeds.

In spite of shearing, the speargrass trouble was no less. Sheep became steadily weaker, many dying each day. Evidently the men did not understand that if they held the sheep on some clean range for a few weeks, the destructive spears would mature and fall to the ground, leaving the trail to the North much safer. As it was, they counted a few dead sheep every day and pushed forward.

On July 7, according to Campbell's journal, the flock was down to six hundred and seventy head, about half of the original band. And on August 25, the count was two hundred and ninety-five.

To add to an already wide variety of troubles, Sioux Indians appeared. They might have been expected to fall unmercifully upon the remaining sheep but, unpredictable as always, they simply gazed in amazement. Rae passed out some gifts and the Natives became friendly, even offered to accompany the white men for some distance to protect them from "bad Indians."

About this time there was another problem; the men ran out of food for themselves. But with some surviving sheep, complete famine was impossible and Campbell mentions killing a sheep "for our kettle." A few days later, at Grand Point, a boat from the settlement met the travellers beside the Red River, delivered provisions for the hungry men and took on the baggage and some lame sheep. That was a relief.

Weary and sick of it all, they were now near home. On September 16, 1833, they drove the band of two hundred and forty-one emaciated and weakened sheep into the Selkirk Settlement and met with both commendation and criticism.

SURE, THE MEN IN CHARGE of the drive made mistakes. At the end of the journey it was easy to see how things could have been improved. They might have bought their sheep in Missouri, even at higher prices, and thus shortened the drive. And, certainly, they should have avoided travelling when the speargrass danger was at the peak of its severity.

The sheep were taken to the Experimental Farm on the Assiniboine, and Robert Campbell was placed in charge. Perhaps this Scot who understood sheep should have been in charge from the beginning. After recovering from the cruel journey, the sheep did well and multiplied. The surviving members of the original flock were undoubtedly the fittest and thus the most appropriate foundation for the pioneer farming colony.

It was sad to think of over a thousand sheep dying on the trail but when everything is considered, it's remarkable that even two hundred and forty-one survived and reached Red River.

English Stallion for Red River

LORD SELKIRK'S MERINO SHEEP, after the long journey from Spain to the point where the city of Winnipeg was to arise, became the West's first farm animals of pure breeding; but two stallions—a Hackney called Fireaway and an English Thoroughbred, Melbourne—were by far the most famous and successful of pedigreed improvers in the pre-railroad years.

And moving imported horses over the seven hundred-mile land and water route from York Factory on Hudson Bay to the Red River was more awkward, more difficult and more dangerous than transporting sheep. Even the most ardent horse lovers will think of adventures more inviting than sharing a canoe or York boat with a frisky stallion, no matter how he might be dignified by fine pedigree.

Horses were native to North America—as natural and wild as bison—but the race became extinct at some time long before the white man arrived. The continent then remained completely horseless until colonizers following Columbus brought Spanish horse-stock with them. From that domestic foundation came the semi-wild mustangs and the stock propagated by Indian tribes. Horses of the new strain appeared in the possession of Snake Indians beside the Bow River about 1730.

AFTER A NOTABLE TRIP through unknown parts of the West in 1755, Fur Trader Anthony Henday returned to York Factory with hard-to-believe tales about his adventures. Having penetrated into what is now Western Alberta, he was the first white man to see the Canadian Rockies and, still more astonishing to his Company friends, to report seeing Indians riding horses. Although his listeners had doubts, Henday was reporting truthfully. Natives of the Blackfoot tribes had recently acquired horses, mainly by theft from their more southerly neighbors. Hence, the white man had nothing to do directly with reintroduction of horses to Western Canada.

The Selkirk Settlers were able to get horses for their immediate requirements from the Natives but, having known the massive and improved breeds of Scotland, England and Ireland, were unimpressed by the small and broken-colored Indian cayuses. These latter were, however, hardy and sure-footed and, as historian Alexander Ross quite correctly said, "their appearance is not prepossessing, but they are better than they look. Few horses could be better adapted for the cart and the saddle, and none so good for the climate."

But the local horses were not appreciated. To most people they were ugly and spiritless. Sharing that view, Governor George Simpson wrote: "Some plan must soon be fallen upon to increase our stock and improve our breed of horses as they are becoming very scarce and of such small growth as to be quite unfit for our work."

"We should select good mares from the United States and from the stock at our own posts," the governor added, "and get a superior stallion from England." The result, he hoped, would be heavier horses for farming, and faster horses for buffalo hunting.

Delivering an English stallion at Red River Colony would present unusual difficulties. But from York Factory Simpson made formal request to Company officers in London, and under date of February 23, 1831, came reply from Deputy Governor Nicholas Garry, "We shall send out a stallion of a proper breed by the Ship to York Factory. We should think the experimental farm at Red River the best place to commence raising horses for the service."

The stallion was the famous Fireaway. On arrival at York Factory in the summer of 1831, he was transferred immediately to one of the oar-propelled York boats used on the route between Hudson Bay and Fort Garry. Hay and oats were carried but there were the many portages, at each of which the horse had to be unloaded and reloaded. It wasn't easy and the horse didn't like it any better than the men who were obliged to sit at the animal's feet. Once the great horse fell out of the boat and swam to shore where he was caught and reloaded.

Notwithstanding the numerous hazards created by a horse struggling constantly to balance himself in such a boat—call it freight canoe or York boat—George Simpson could report, ultimately, to London that the stallion "reached the settlement in perfect safety ... and will soon give us a better breed of horses. He is looked upon as one of the wonders of the world by the natives, many of whom have travelled great distances with no other object than to see him."

As for the horse's type and performance, Robert Campbell who was at the Experimental Farm when Fireaway was there said, "He was a splendid bright bay, standing 16 hands and very stoutly built, with a faultless shape. He was warranted to trot fifteen miles an hour and could do much better."

For the breeding season following, twenty-five selected mares were brought from the Athabasca River to Fort Garry and twenty-five from Fort Carlton—long trail trips by any standards.

In due course there were foals bearing the clear marks of superiority; and in the years that followed, the maturing Fireaway horses came to be regarded as the swiftest buffalo runners and the most useful road horses in the country. Even the Indians, reveling in the delights of horsestealing, made it their highest ambition to acquire the sons and daughters of Fireaway.

Where did the famous stallion go ultimately? On that point there was speculation. According to one story, he was sold to a United States buyer; another report told of the horse being

stolen and whisked across the boundary, and still another, that
his breeding worth became so well established that he was taken
back by way of Hudson Bay to England where he was used to
produce steeple chasers.

>─┤◆>─○─◆┤─<

IN ANY CASE, FIREAWAY PASSED INTO HISTORY and the Hudson's
Bay Company, satisfied with the result of the first effort in horse
improvement, agreed to secure and send another stallion. In
May, 1848, Captain Pelly was authorized to buy the English
Thoroughbred, Melbourne, at a price of two hundred and ten
pounds. At the same time, a Thoroughbred mare was purchased,
also a bull and two cows of Ayrshire breed. Bluebloods all, they
went forward in the sailing vessel, Prince Rupert, bound for
York Factory. In charge of the stock was Thomas Howsom Axe,
"a skilful groom" engaged for three years at thirty pounds per
year with a bonus of five pounds if all the purebred animals were
delivered in good health at York Factory.

Axe qualified for his bonus, and James Hargrave's entry in
the York Factory journal on August 28, 1848, tells of four York
boats leaving at noon for Red River Settlement "laden with the
horse and mare, bull and two cows received by Prince Rupert
... The live stock were amply supplied with oatmeal for the
voyage (there being no oats at the factory) and the horses with
oil cloth covers in addition to the horse cloths brought from
England, while the groom in charge was furnished with sickles,
ropes and utensils considered necessary for their proper security during the voyage."

After three weeks of rowing and portaging in daylight hours
and worrying about tether ropes at night, Mr. Mowat and his
crew brought the brigade of boats bearing the purebreds to the
north end of Lake Winnipeg. Chief Factor Donald Ross
watched the boats depart from Norway House and noted in a
letter that "the live stock from Europe" made a "troublesome
and dangerous cargo." At the same time, he expressed a prayer-
ful hope that all might be brought safely to the settlement.

Mr. Mowat's boats suffered some damage from sharp hoofed feet but, otherwise, the "troublesome and dangerous cargo" was delivered safely and Chief Factor Alexander Christie at Lower Fort Garry was pleased with the stock, as he was with the immigrant caretaker who appeared to be a "decent industrious man—and apparently well qualified for the duty for which he was engaged."

Here then were the first Thoroughbred horses and the first purebred cattle of any breed in Rupert's Land, and Christie recommended that they be kept at Red River Settlement where twenty cows were already gathered for breeding to the new bull, and to which place twenty of the best mares would be brought from Fort Pelly.

The grey Thoroughbred mare dropped a foal in the following spring and Fort Garry interest soared. But there were bad days ahead. During the breeding season, Melbourne kicked the good groom, breaking the man's arm. Later in the season, the mare and foal died and Eden Colvile, Acting Governor of Rupert's Land wrote to Sir George Simpson, confessing an opinion that the purebred animals were a poor speculation. The stallion, Melbourne, he advised, should be sent to St. Louis and "sold for what he will fetch."

But the advice to sell the stallion was not accepted. After a few years, Melbourne was taken to Fort Pelly, by trail of course, and used extensively at that point which became the Company's chief horse breeding station. Most of Melbourne's colts were bright bays like himself and, generally of good quality.

Never, however, did the sons and daughters of Melbourne attain the degree of fame and popularity enjoyed by Fireaway offspring. For 50 years the settlers talked about the speed and endurance of Fireaway stock. A horse known to be a great-grandson or great-granddaughter of Fireaway was likely to command a substantially better price than a horse of equal quality and unknown breeding.

AS LATE AS 1877, settlers in the Portage la Prairie area revived their affection for the memory of that horse which was the first purebred of his race in all of Western Canada. A stranger driving a fast horse blew into town a day or two before the 24th of May and promptly challenged all comers to a matched race. With the honor of the community and the reputation of local horses at stake, townsmen came together for serious discussion. Settlers with swift horses were remembered, and thoughts turned to Farmer John Macdonald at High Bluff who had a nimble great-great-granddaughter of Fireaway. A message was dispatched: "Bring your mare to town at once. We need her for a race."

Macdonald was plowing with a two-horse team when the exhausted courier reached him. Reluctantly, he unhitched the good mare and her mate from the walking plow, rehitched them to his democrat and drove to Portage. Farmers and town people couldn't honestly expect a homesteader's plowhorse to win a race against a barnstorming flier from St. Paul but they recalled her breeding and nursed a silent hope. It was a great race; every pioneer who saw it agreed and, sure enough, the blood of Fireaway was still virile if not invincible and Macdonald's mare, drawing a farm democrat and an exultant Scottish settler, came down the Portage la Prairie street to leave the professional racer from Minnesota a convincing distance behind.

Men talked again about the greatness of Fireaway but forgotten were the heroic men who accepted the nigh frightening task of bringing stallions from Hudson Bay to the present location of Winnipeg when there was no means of transportation better than a freight canoe.

Longhorns and Shorthorns
of Manitoba Trails

THE LAND ACT OF 1872, providing for homesteading in the Northwest, was like a spark setting the stubble ablaze. No railroad had penetrated to any part of the new country—nor would one be built for another six years—but settlers couldn't wait. Inspired by the promise of free land and virgin fertility, they came into Winnipeg by riverboat and on foot, and usually continued westward by oxcart.

Winnipeg was the gateway to the new empire and as human population began to rise there and in the homestead country, shifts and readjustments in cattle holdings became necessary to meet the changing demands for food and breeding stock.

Cattlemen thought little of placing herds on the trails. If livestock in numbers had to be moved, there was no alternative to driving—a case of one long day after another and often in the most disagreeable weather. Most herds seen on Manitoba trails at that time were small ones, admittedly, some consisting merely of the three of four cows being driven ahead of carts by settlers making their way to new homesteads. But a few were big enough to attract attention anywhere, like the six hundred and seventy-head herd brought to Winnipeg from the South in 1876 and mentioned by Alexander Begg in his book, *Ten Years In Winnipeg*. And certain other trail herds—Adam MacKenzie's Shorthorns for example—exerted most important influences upon the quality and character of cattle across the entire province of Manitoba in the years following.

Moreover, there were trail herds in that period when the prairie buffalo population was declining rapidly which proved to be the means of preventing serious local food famines. In the early winter of 1876-77, famine threatened the little community at Fort Livingstone, capital for a brief period of the Northwest Territories. There, on a rise of ground overlooking the valley of Swan River, the Mounted Police built in 1874 and it suited Ottawa's convenience to use the facilities as a seat of government for the Territories.

Preparations were being made for the first session of the Council of the Northwest Territories and everything except the necessary food supplies seemed to be in hand. Lieutenant-Governor Laird would preside and Colonel James F. Macleod, Commissioner of the Northwest Mounted Police and one of the appointed members of the Council, was making the long and tedious trip from Fort Macleod. Leaving Fort Macleod in early December, the Commission went by trail to Fort Benton in Montana, thence to Helena, Bismark, Moorhead and Winnipeg. Finally, from the Manitoba metropolis he travelled by dog-team to Livingstone.

It was severely cold when Colonel Macleod reached the "capital," and wood was being cut and hauled to supply ninety stoves in use by mounted police, government servants and the few people with uncertain purpose. But the worry about food shortage had ended; the cattle from Battleford, three hundred lonely miles to the west, had arrived.

Acting Constable Beaudieu and a half-breed helper, driving the thirty head of essential meat animals, encountered the onset of an early winter, causing delay and the anxiety over rations at Fort Livingstone. That drive, occupying somewhat more than a month, was by way of Fort Carlton and the Touchwood Trail; and there was the South Saskatchewan River to swim before the ice formed on it.

Winnipeg people at that time saw herds being driven from south of the boundary rather often. The local press with limited domestic news, reported cattle movements and the arrival of steamboats on the Red River with diligence. In the *Daily Free Press* of September 21, 1875, there was an account of a herd driven from St. Cloud, Minnesota, about three hundred miles: "Mr. E. Cross of St. Cloud, Minnesota, arrived on Tuesday with one hundred head of cattle for which he is finding good sale, beef cattle being disposed of at three and one-half to four cents live weight. Mr. Clarke of the firm of Clarke and McClure, will arrive tomorrow with two hundred head of Texas cattle, a portion of a lot he purchased in Kansas. The balance of the lot are now at Bismark."

On August 22, 1879, the *Winnipeg Weekly Times* reported that, "One hundred and seventy-five head of cattle from Minnesota passed down Main Street about noon on Tuesday and attracted considerable attention. They were driven down Point Douglas Avenue and all swam the Red River successfully." And as proof of some incoming herds of the period being really immense, there is the testimony of Alexander Begg that T. J. Demers had arrived from French-town, Montana, "bringing with him a herd of six hundred and seventy cattle."

>-!-‹›-•-O-‹•›-!-‹

BUT OF ALL THE LIVESTOCK driven to Manitoba in the decade, it was the MacKenzie Shorthorns which had the best claim to a place of distinction in the annals of agriculture. Adam MacKenzie, 23 years old and about as robust as a range-raised yearling bull, was coming from Puslinch, Ontario, to join his father on land ten miles west of Portage la Prairie. In was the year 1871, and the young fellow could enjoy the comforts of train travel as far as St. Paul, Minnesota. Had it not been for the herd of Shorthorns he was bringing to Manitoba, he might have travelled part of the remaining distance on a Red River steamboat, but with a herd of Ontario cattle in his care, he had no choice but to accept the hardships and uncertainties of five hundred miles of trail between St. Paul and Portage la Prairie.

There was at least one purebred Shorthorn bull in Manitoba before that date—one registered as Solway and brought by Adam's father, Kenneth MacKenzie, when he came in 1868. But the cows being directed across the plains by the younger MacKenzie may have been the first purebred females of their breed in the West.

Of course, this man chasing pedigreed cattle over an expanse of country still frequented by buffalo and mischief-bent Sioux Indians was not one to turn his back on anything because it was difficult, as the events of subsequent years showed most clearly. Manitoba pioneers remembered him as one who became the biggest farm operator of his generation. At a time when municipal administration allowed farmers to defray part of their land taxes by doing one day of "road work" for every quarter section standing in their respective names on the assessment list, Adam MacKenzie was said to have had enough farm property to keep one man and team going every working day throughout the year.

In starting a herd of cattle northward from St. Paul at that particular time, young MacKenzie had nothing to guide him except a good sense of direction and some well defined cart ruts cut in the sod. Branching tracks could be confusing but the deepest ruts were the ones to follow in this instance because they were the ones made by the Red River cart trains which ground their way over the shortest route between St. Paul and Fort Garry for many years.

A "train" on that trail consisted of as many as five hundred carts in a long and dusty procession, the raucous shrieks from wheels turning on dry axels being audible for miles. Even with the growth of riverboat service on the Red River, a great many carts and freight wagons were still in use when Adam MacKenzie and his cattle made their way northward.

While driving over this country which was completely new and strange to him, MacKenzie had none of the aids and conveniences like saddle horses and cowboy assistants. He was alone and had the added encumbrance of a team of heavy and hairy-legged horses hitched to a wagon loaded high with equipment for the farm. It meant that when contrary cattle chose to leave the trail, MacKenzie was obliged to follow them with the team and wagon or leave the outfit on the road and pursue the wayward beasts on foot.

The most trying part of the trip followed immediately upon departure from St. Paul. Throughout the first few days, uncooperative Ontario cattle, perhaps confused by the limitless sweep of unfenced country, insisted upon striking out aimlessly in senseless directions. The man urgently needed a good stockhorse. In the first days it became necessary for him to unhitch the team periodically, tie one horse to a wagon wheel, mount the other and conduct a miniature round-up. After getting the cattle back on the trail and driving them for a mile or two in the proper direction, he would return to the wagon at a gallop, hitch and drive on to overtake the herd. Not only was it difficult for the man but it was hard on the horse which had to perform double service.

The trail went by St. Cloud, at which point MacKenzie and his cattle turned their backs on the Mississippi River and drove toward Moorhead on the east side of the Red. From that point, the route to Winnipeg was directly north—except for the inevitable twists and turns in every primitive trail.

When it rained, Adam MacKenzie was exposed to it all; when the sun went down, he spread his blankets on the ground beside or beneath the wagon; when the mosquitos and flies attacked, there was pandemonium beside the river, and when mounted Indians with scalping knives suspended recklessly by thongs from their belts, blocked the trail, the young man had visions of painful disaster. But one by one the trails passed and the end of an even month after leaving St. Paul found MacKenzie and his charges at the mouth of the Assiniboine River, ready for the final four-day or five-day drive westward to Rat Creek.

"Ye've done weel, lad," was the fond greeting from the Highland-accented elder MacKenzie; "o, course, a MacKenzie should ne've dae less." It was good to be at journey's end and survey the new home beyond which, westward, there were no known neighbors. The two horses were tired but the cattle were in good condition and the herd was enlarged by calves born on the trail. Seed stock, superior seed stock for the new farming country, was delivered. And one year later, when Portage la Prairie held the first agricultural fair on the Prairies—still two years before the Mounted Police made their historic trek to establish a post in the far West—some of the Shorthorns driven from St. Paul were class winners.

>-+-+>-O-<+-+-<

MANY OF THE CATTLE brought to Winnipeg and elsewhere in the North at that time were extremely long in their horns, obviously not far removed in time and breeding from the Spanish stock propagating like wild animals on grassy plains near the Gulf of Mexico. Cattle driven from the South had two or three purposes. Some were slaughtered on arrival to furnish beef for the growing Winnipeg population. Many were sold to incoming settlers for breeding purposes and a few of the steers were given some superficial and inadequate lessons in wearing harness or yokes and sold as work oxen to unsuspecting landseekers in urgent need of power. A homesteader at Indian Head drove two spotted oxen whose slabsided conformation and great length of horns made it reasonably clear that either they or their mothers travelled the longest cattle trail in the world—from the Rio Grande by way of Dodge City and Bismark to Winnipeg, and then to Indian Head, Northwest Territories.

The cow stock driven from the South was ugly by usual standards but it was hardy and, mated to bulls from the MacKenzie Shorthorns or other improved breeds, gave the homestead country a useful type of cattle. And cattle a few generations removed from the Longhorn cows with hooves worn thin from much trail travel produced market toppers and some show champions.

Cattle on Mountain Trails

IT WAS THE GOLD RUSH to Fraser River and Cariboo that drew men like Lewis "Shifty" Campbell and "Gypsy" Johnny Wilson to the good inter-mountain grass and gave cattle raising in the British Columbia Interior its initial impetus.

News of gold on the river produced the usual frenzied rush. Men lured by the winsomeness of a gamble—willing to risk their very lives for a longshot chance of fortune—converged upon the river and, later, William Creek. Twenty-five thousand miners had to be fed and, fortunately, there were men possessing that extra measure of pertinacity needed to take cattle and sheep over the hundreds of miles of untravelled mountain country.

The nearest supply of cattle was in the Valley of the Columbia River in Oregon Territory. To that part the Hudson's Bay Company brought California cattle and encouraged breeding before the Oregon Treaty of 1846 fixed the boundary and placed what had been a "no-man's-land" securely within the ownership of United States. Cattle multiplied and prices for surplus stock were low enough to attract speculators. But the stark task of driving a herd beyond the unpredictable obstacles of Okanagan and Cariboo Trails was something to fill all but the most foolhardy mortals with terror.

THE FIRST ADVENTURER to take cattle and other provisions over the barrier-strewn route to the mines was Joel Palmer, later superintendent of Indian Affairs for Oregon, member of the State Legislature and unsuccessful Republican candidate for governor. Following him were trail-broken cattlemen like John Jeffries who drove herds from the Dalles to the Fraser River in each of several years; Joe Greaves who brought size and distinction to the Douglas Lake Ranch; Jerome and Thaddeus Harper who founded the mighty Gang Ranch and other British Columbia cattle enterprises, and those extraordinary cattlemen—Campbell and Wilson—whose ultimate experience made them at home on any mountain trail, like cats in a slaughterhouse.

Blazing trails was not new for Joel Palmer. From his home in Indiana, he had gone overland to Oregon Territory in 1845 and the journal written on that trip became the acknowledged guide book for immigrants following him. On the initial drive from Oregon to the North—in 1858—he was leaving the Dalles in June with nine wagons, each drawn by six or eight oxen. Crossing the International Boundary near Osoyoos, he directed his outfit along a pack trail on the west side of Okanagan Lake and through Kamloops to Bonaparte Creek where he slaughtered the oxen and sold the beef and other supplies to men on their way to the mines. In early June of the next year, Palmer was again driving through Kamloops, this time with 100 mules and the provisions he considered most urgently needed by the miners, specifically cattle and whisky.

But in catching a vision of cattle raising in this new and inhospitable country, and acting upon it, who were ahead of the two-fisted Lewis Campbell and square-jawed Johnny Wilson? Who, indeed, knew more about the early cattle trails connecting the Interior with the outside—south to Oregon, north to remote mining communities and west to the Pacific Coast?

Campbell and Wilson were not the first to drive cattle to the Interior, true enough, but they were probably the first to take breeding stock, and Dr. Lawrence Guichon believes they were the first to drive surplus cattle from the region of Kamloops to the Coast.

In England where he was born to Gypsy parents, Johnny Wilson roamed the countryside while members of the nomadic band practiced the arts of telling fortunes, trading horses and sharpening knives and scissors. But with thoughts of bigger things, the Gypsy boy of 17 years left the relatively uneventful life of his people, crossed the Atlantic and engaged as a farm helper in Indiana. The farmer's name was Campbell, and he had a son, Lewis, just one year older than Wilson. Though differing greatly in temperament and integrity, the two boys were attracted to each other. Together they talked about going west. When stories reached them about gold discoveries in California, they resolved to go. Fate took them by different routes, however; Campbell who later became known by the unflattering name of "Shifty," went by wagon road across half a continent and Wilson took ship to the Isthmus of Panama and up the west coast to San Francisco.

As in the experience of most men who joined one gold rush or another in history, California held no fortune for these two. Nevertheless, when the rush was on to the Fraser River in 1858, their urge was to try again. Northward they made their way. Working separately for several years they prospected, mined and peddled the beef from worn-out oxen, all without more than meagre reward. In 1861, Campbell was wintering oxen and pack mules beside Bonaparte Creek, close to the Cariboo Trail, and in the next year he was working on the Fraser River when a group of those celebrated people known as the Overlanders floated by, not sure where they would stop or what dangers lay ahead.

>-·-◆-·-O-·-◆-·-<

THEN FOR CAMPBELL AND WILSON, fortunes improved. Campbell brought in a herd of slaughter cattle—chased it over the trails from somewhere south of the line—and made a handsome profit. Wilson, simultaneously, struck rich ore in his Tinker Mine on Williams Creek. Though working quite independently, it was now in the minds of both men to quit the mining and trading, and turn to cattle raising. By 1864, the big Campbell—six feet tall and muscular—was settling down on a place favored with good bunchgrass, Campbell's Creek, about twelve miles east of Kamloops. It was a place he had chosen in the first instance for its suitability in running work oxen. There Wilson found him and made his proposal: pool resources and drive a herd of cattle from the South—for breeding. "It's time this country was raising its own cattle," he argued; "that good grass will carry them as well as anything in Oregon."

Campbell was not difficult to convince and before the snow had melted in the spring of 1865, the two men were riding south, Wilson carrying the bag of gold dust with which to pay for the cattle they would buy, and Campbell carrying the guns for use in case of threat to the gold. Wilson with his Gypsy training was the better bargainer and Campbell, by reputation, was the handier with firearms. The arrangement worked well and in Oregon where cattle were available for purchase, Wilson negotiated the deals. In the country south of Umatilla, the new herd was assembled—three hundred head.

The long drive began—cattle, mounted men and an ox-drawn wagon conveying the supplies. The trail touched the Columbia River at a point west of Walla Walla, crossed the Snake River and twisted northward on the east side of the Columbia for a couple hundred miles to Fort Okanagan. At that point, cattle and cattlemen forded or swam the big river and continued on the west side of Okanagan River.

McLaughlin's Canyon reminded these and all travellers of a savage battle between Indians and whites. Young Natives were still resentful and plotted to cut out some cattle from passing herds or cut the throats of the cattlemen. On that section of trail in Northern Washington, the good Chief Tonasket provided the cattlemen with an escort to see them well along the Okanagan River where "the bad Indians" roamed.

At the Similkameen River there was the crossing to consider and at Osoyoos, the International Boundary and customs duty. But the fact of being on British soil made the way no easier. Along the trail were the marks of campsites used by cattlemen taking herds to the mines, and Campbell could recall the drives made by John Jeffries, Major Thorp, Henry Cock and others. It was there on the Canadian portion of the trail that Cock was robbed. One of his own party of cattlemen was suspected and, while cattle rested, a trial was conducted before a six-man home-spun jury. Campbell, it seems, was either a juror or a spectator. Evidence was inconclusive but the suspect failed to explain convincingly how he happened to come by some recently acquired wealth. The jurors, lacking better reason, ruled that the man had the face of a thief and if he wasn't guilty of this crime, probably he was guilty of another and should be hung. The rope was being prepared when John McLean, retired from the office of Hudson's Bay factor at Kamloops, came that way and protested that no man was ever hung on such flimsy pretext in British Territory. The man was released.

❯━┥◆┝━O━┥◆┝━❮

IT WAS A FIVE-DAY TRIP along the west side of Okanagan Lake— the Great Lake as it was known. The way was described as rough and mountainous but no Ogopogo lake serpents were reported. From the top end of the lake, the way went west through a belt of forest, then open country known as Grand Prairie; and at last the cattle were given freedom on the grass beside Campbell's Creek, east of Kamloops. Had the herd been intended for the mines, it would have been driven west from Kamloops to ford or swim the Thompson River at the place occupied by a French Canadian known as Savona. There Savona operated a ferry for ordinary traffic but for herds of cattle he could offer nothing better than a place to wade the broad stream.

The Campbell-Wilson drive was a success. For a time the two men ran their cattle together but Wilson, knowing "Shifty's" reputation, decided to conduct his breeding operations at a safe distance. He took his cattle to Eight Mile Creek, near Ashcroft.

But as the three hundred head of Oregon cattle came up the valley to Campbell's Creek, things were beginning to change.

Many miners realized they could make more money in wages by chopping wood back home, and the population up Barkerville way began to decline. The demand for beef dwindled and gradually the growing herds like those of Campbell and Wilson were able to meet the need. The driving of slaughter cattle from United States territory practically ceased in 1868; the last big herd had come north and there was the immediate prospect of the flow being reversed.

There was still no prospect of railroad and for those two robust cattlemen who believed that cattle held a better future than gold, three possible outlets existed, all of them difficult. Surplus cattle might be driven back down the Okanagan Trail and sold in the United States; secondly, there was a chance of selling at New Westminster or Victoria, and, finally, some small waves of gold seekers were still going into remote parts of the North, far beyond Barkerville, stubborn men yet hoping to find their fortunes.

Not once but many times both Wilson and Campbell drove cattle south over the old Hudson's Bay Company Brigade Trail through Merritt and on by the Princeton-Hope Trail to Hope where, with luck, they'd connect with a river boat going to New Westminster and Victoria. And if there was no boat, the alternative was to drive all the way.

Campbell, to be sure, was the first to extend the northern drives far beyond Barkerville and, fortunately, his great drive to Dease Lake is at least noted and dated by the Kamloops Sentinel of January 7, 1898. For the benefit of the editor, Lewis Campbell related driving one hundred and twenty-five cattle from Kamloops to Dease Lake in 1874, leaving Kamloops on April 25 and arriving at the Lake—close to the present north boundary of British Columbia—where there was a spell of mining activity, in exactly four months. The newspaper note coincided with interest in taking beef to Dawson City and the editor added, "Mr. Campbell is feeding fifteen hundred head of cattle on his ranch near Kamloops, most of which will be driven north during the season of 1898."

Campbell remained at Campbell's Creek. Wilson acquired one ranch after another, among them a place at Savona and one at Grand Prairie, or Westwold as it was known later. Both old trail drivers became Cattle Kings in their Interior. Dying at Eight Mile Creek in 1904, "Gypsy" Johnny left forty-four hundred cattle and "Shifty" Campbell, going down the same Long Trail six years later, left twenty-five hundred cattle. Both men had seen a dream come true.

"We'll Drive 'Em to San Francisco"

>–!–‹›–☉–‹›–!–‹

DISTANCE MEANT NOTHING TO THE HARPERS—Jerome and younger brother Thaddeus. They'd undertake a trip of a thousand miles about as readily as one of a hundred. If volume of trail activity were measured in cow-miles, the Harpers would have no rivals for the Canadian record—unless it was in Tom Lynch who drove numerous herds to the foothills.

Regardless of who may have preceded them in driving herds to the inter-mountain sections of British Columbia, the Harpers managed to make an especially big share of cattle history in that part. And in completing the unequalled cattle drive from the British Columbia Interior to San Francisco, Thaddeus Harper deserves the historian's special accolade. By the route over which he guided the big herd of Canadian cattle, it was no less than two thousand miles—the rough equivalent of starting from the Stampede Grounds at Calgary and terminating at Maple Leaf Gardens in Toronto.

The Harpers were Virginians by birth and throughout their hard and eventful lives they spoke with typical softness in accent and retained their native sentiment for the things of the Old South. When Civil War was in progress, the brothers were driving beef herds to Barkerville but, eager to help the southern cause, they took steps to outfit a raiding vessel at Victoria, the idea being to send it against shipping out of San Francisco. Such an ambitious expression of feeling was proof at least that the cattle trade about Barkerville was proving profitable.

As young men craving adventure, the brothers crossed the continent with a wave of gold-seekers bound for California and from there they went to the Fraser River. But with above-average business judgment, they devoted their time to sawmill operation, road construction and finally the beef trade, leaving the less profitable toil with pans and shovels to others.

><+>•O•<+•><

GOLD DISCOVERY ON WILLIAM'S CREEK—called after William Dietz—was in 1861. A year later Billy Barker made a rich strike in a shaft near the site on which the roaring town of Barkerville was built—and the great rush was on. The Harpers, by this time, were making their way from Oregon and Washington with four hundred cattle, including a few milk cows for sale along the route. Like others taking American cattle to the mines, they crossed near Osoyoos, followed the Okanagan Trail to Kamloops, drove west to cross the Thompson River at Savona and continued north on the old Cariboo Trail.

It was hard travelling. Indians were only a little less unfriendly than the mountain grizzlies, and the rocks under foot were sharp and treacherous. But at Barkerville, after many weeks on the trail, there was double reward: a market created by beef-hungry miners and the experience of a story-book community where fortunes were made and squandered with commonplace frequency. Most of the half million dollars Billy Barker was supposed to have taken from his claim was spent at the bar; and one known as Red McMartin, according to a story, went into a saloon with $40,000 in his pockets and maintained an unbroken orgy of drinking, treating, and furniture destruction until he walked out penniless.

But beef commanded seventy-five cents a pound; every critter brought up the trail in the Harper band was like a small fortune in a cowhide. The cattle were herded wherever there was grass, a few head being cut out for slaughter each day.

Before the last steer was butchered, the Harpers were on their way south for another herd. Obviously, the enterprise was profitable. Early in the spring of 1863, they were again on their way northward, ready to move into British territory in May. Jerome, the more shrewd and voluble of the brothers rode ahead and at Kamloops met the well-publicized world travellers, Viscount Milton and Dr. Cheadle, adventuresome Englishmen who had been hunting buffalo on the plains in the previous year and were now enroute to the Cariboo.

Dr. Cheadle's journal entry of September 2, 1863, made when at Kamloops, tells about his meeting with the cattlemen: "In the afternoon a Mr. Jerome Harper arrived on horseback; he is bringing in a drove of five hundred cattle from Oregon; a Virginian and staunch supporter of the South. He treated us to a tremendous tirade against the North, whom he called by all the vile names he could think of, hoped every Yankee would leave his bones on Southern soil; South would never be conquered; if they were, North would then set upon England whom they hated as heartily as they did the South. Said he was bitter because his mother and family had been driven out of their homes in Virginia where they had nice estates and left penniless."

Once more the Harper cattle were driven west to connect with the Cariboo Trail, witnessing in that year the strangest collection of vehicles in the world—everything from a mule-powered freight wagon which rattled over the rocks to the two specially constructed wheelbarrows that three robust prospectors were using to transport eight hundred pounds of provisions from Yale to Quesnel.

That drive like the previous Harper effort was rewarding, and others followed until the brothers dominated the beef business at the mines. There was just one unfortunate feature—the demand couldn't last long. But like Lewis Campbell and Johnny Wilson, the Harpers were convinced that cattle could be raised on the northern grass. Accordingly, about the time of the first drive, the brothers acquired land on the South Thompson, east of Kamloops. The land, incidentally, is still known as Harper Ranch.

⊱┈◆┈○┈◆┈⊰

IT IS IMPOSSIBLE TO KNOW exactly when the Harpers decided to breed cattle on the Canadian side, but when discouraged miners were leaving the Cariboo, the brothers were left with a couple hundred head of unsold cattle—not worth driving back to Oregon. Most spectators doubted if there would ever be another market in the North or if cattle were worth the trouble of branding. It would have been easy and perhaps logical for the Harpers to abandon the animals, take a loss on the last drive and return to live in a more civilized part of the world. But they shared a premonition that their cattle would become saleable sooner or later; they branded everything capable of breeding and again released the cattle to rustle, some in the Cariboo, some east of Kamloops.

For a few years the cattle business felt serious depression, just as the cynics had prophesied. But the Harpers remained and now and then drove a few head to the coast to sell at New Westminster or Victoria or Nanaimo. In 1870, the enterprising Jerome became ill, retired to California and died there four years later, age forty-eight. Thaddeus was left to count the cattle periodically, brand the calves and hope for the realization of a market.

The cattle multiplied, exactly as cattle were supposed to do, and Thaddeus regularly gathered the wild things from mountain sides and valleys and marked them with the JH brand, fashioned from Jerome's initials. By the spring of 1876, Thaddeus concluded the necessity of a bold move. "I'm going to take a few hundred of these steers somewhere," he said to a Kamloops man.

"But there's no place to take them," came the reply. "They wouldn't eat all your cattle at New Westminster in a year; and Chicago's too far, even if you knew how to get there."

"Chicago!" exclaimed Harper; "that's an idea. I always wanted to see Chicago anyway. I'll tell you all about the place when I get back."

By mid-April the plans were made and the *British Colonist* published in Victoria reported on April 20, 1876: "Mr. T. Harper proposes to take eight hundred head of beef cattle from British Columbia to Chicago. He intends to drive via Salt Lake and then take the railroad. At present there are a large number of cattle in the Interior; the market is limited and a band of beef cattle would hardly realize fifteen dollars per head. At present, at Chicago, cattle will net over the cost of driving and railroad expense about forty dollars a head. A few shipments to that point would tend to relieve the market in the Interior and consequently give stock-owners a better opportunity of disposing of their cattle."

Cattle for the journey were gathered in the Cariboo and started south on the Cariboo Trail. It resembled some of the Harper drives of a decade or more before, except that the herd was bigger and the direction reversed.

The *British Colonist* of Sunday, May 21, 1876, reported herd progress thus: "Our informant met Harper's band of cattle—some eight hundred head—on Tuesday last, a little above Clinton, bound for Salt Lake City. A few of the animals looked poor but the majority were good beeves."

The herd was forced across the Thompson at Savona and driven on to Kamloops where an additional four hundred head of Harper cattle from the nearby range were added, making twelve hundred cattle in all. Of course, Harper was accompanying the herd and with him were eight or nine riders, one of them being twenty-two-year-old Antoine Allen who had come from Oregon as a boy and lived with the Harpers. All riders were well armed, Allen explained, and anticipated the necessity of using their guns.

>─┼─◇─○─◇─┼─<

IT WAS A BIG HERD—the biggest ever seen on the Okanagan Trail—and travel was only ten or twelve miles a day. But nobody was in a hurry and cattle and cattlemen made their way across the International Boundary, across the State of Washington, across a portion of Oregon, across Idaho and into Northern Utah where Harper believed it a good place to winter. The general idea was still to drive to rail-head as soon as the cattle had time to recover some condition on spring grass, and ship to Chicago. But during the winter a traveller with wagon and team of mules came that way and expressed the opinion that, with drought in California, the British Columbia cattle would probably bring a better price in San Francisco than in Chicago.

"Do you think so?" Harper enquired with obvious interest. "Then we'll drive 'em to San Francisco."

In the spring, instead of heading toward the railhead, Harper turned the herd westward, drove across the States of Nevada and California, across mountainous country, Indian country, dry country, all new and strange to him. And eighteen months after leaving the Cariboo, Harper and his men drove the big herd into San Francisco and could report no more losses than would be expected in a herd of twelve hundred cattle.

From the *British Colonist* of February 5, 1878, one may read, "Some eighteen months ago Mr. Thaddeus Harper drove from British Columbia into Northern Idaho twelve hundred head of beef cattle ... Now Mr. Harper's band is coming into market at San Francisco. The cattle are large and well grown beeves, rolling in fat, and have been sold at seventy dollars per head."

Some of the steers were offered as trained oxen, "larger and finer than anything usually found in California."

As one tries to assess it now, Harper's cattle drive from British Columbia to San Francisco must be seen as one of the most notable in the history of agriculture. Had it originated in Texas, no doubt the world would have heard more about it in story and song.

>─◆>─○─<◆─◁

HARPER RETURNED TO BRITISH COLUMBIA, expanded his ranch holdings, and founded the famous Gang Ranch among others.

But Thaddeus lacked the business skill of his brother Jerome and suffered one financial reverse after another. Having lost heavily in the severe winter of 1886–1887, his position deteriorated rapidly and the *Calgary Tribune* of Sept. 5, 1888, tells that, "Thaddeus Harper, a well known stockman of British Columbia, has assigned for the benefit of his creditors." Ten years later, he died at Victoria. He was sixty-nine years of age. T. D. Galpin of London, England, took over the Harper Ranch holdings and organized the Western Canadian Ranching Company. The Harpers were gone but the robust spirit of the men and memory of their courage lingered.

The Trail from Stowaway to Cattle King

>─◄♦►─○─◄♦►─◄

DID JOSEPH BLACKBOURNE GREAVES of Douglas Lake Ranch fame drive four thousand cattle from British Columbia to Cheyenne, Wyoming, as the late Thomas Stewart contended or was the story a simple figment of somebody's imagination as certain individuals chose to conclude? If United States markets existed for B.C. cattle in 1880, who was more likely to organize a gigantic drive than that man who chased sheep up the Cariboo Trail in 1859 and often trailed cattle from Kamloops to the Pacific coast?

In spite of critics, Stewart, who drew upon the experiences of many years as a Douglas Lake Ranch hand and close association with Greaves before becoming Livestock Promoter in Federal government service, contributed the best accounts of the distinguished rancher's early career. And at least one of those who challenged Stewart's account of Greave's pioneer activities, later offered written apology. Much, indeed, that is contained in this chapter was drawn from personal correspondence with the late Tom Stewart.

>─◄♦►─○─◄♦►─◄

With or without the particular cattle drive around which controversy was to turn, the story of Greave's career—from stowaway immigrant to ranchland leader—is worthy of record. Life for him began in Yorkshire, England, in 1831. There was little or no chance of schooling and, if Tom Stewart's information is correct, the boy ran away from home, step-mother and England at the tender age of eleven years. It was then that he stowed away on the sailing ship *Patrick Henry*, bound—as it happened—for New York.

Discovered on board after the boat's departure, the frightened young fellow was brought before an angry captain and ordered by way of punishment to take over all the work in caring for the ship's pigs, which where carried to eat up food refuse and furnish fresh pork when needed. The lad knew nothing about animals but the pigs in the following weeks received undivided attention; and when the *Patrick Henry* docked at New York after a sixty-day voyage, young Greaves could pose as an expert in the art of feeding swine and hired at once with a nearby farmer who owned a barn full of the animals.

That job lasted for three years and there were others. In 1850 he was in St. Louis, Missouri, joining a wagon train going to California. There being safety in numbers in Indian country, prospectors and settlers were glad to join forces—pool their guns, as it were—and this particular cavalcade included sixty-five men, five hundred horses, many wagons and one thousand cattle.

Crossing the States of Missouri, Kansas, Nebraska, Wyoming, Utah, Nevada and on to Sacramento County, California—with mountains added for interest—took months but the trip was concluded with no more than the expected number of scares from truculent Indians and hardships on the trail. In California where gold rush fever gripped most men, Greaves worked as a laborer and then embarked upon a butcher business which was to prove most useful in his later career with cattle.

Came word of gold on the Fraser River and red-blooded frontiersmen wanted to go. Greaves would go too but, with a butcher's reasoning, he decided to take meat animals instead of shovels. He'd take sheep, of all things. It was 1859 and poor trails and rough water still offered the only means of transportation. The flock was bought in Oregon and trailed from a point near the Dalles to Olympia on the coast, not far south of Seattle. There, by waiting a few days, Greaves was able to secure space for himself and his sheep on a boat that would thread its way out of Pudget Sound and into the Fraser River. The advantage was in saving time.

By water Greaves' sheep were taken to Yale, as far as any skipper dared take his boat against a river whose mood became violent above that point.

><->-O-<+>-<

AGAIN MAN AND SHEEP took to what was called a trail—rough surface flattered by such a term. For sixty miles northward to Lytton the way led along the Fraser Gorge, its waters boiling madly. The trail went on to Cache Creek and still generally northward to One Hundred and Fifty Mile House where Greaves sold the sheep for immediate slaughter, sold them at prices which would be unheard of in Oregon and California. But after trailing the flock for two hundred miles before loading it on the boat at Olympia, and about two hundred and fifty miles from Yale—four hundred and fifty miles in all—some special reward would not seem out of place.

Having sold his livestock to advantage, Greaves did what other enterprising men would consider doing; he went back for more. The next time, he brought cattle, drove them the total distance from Oregon by way of Okanagan and Kamloops; then did it again. But on the third trip with cattle, in 1863, he found the market failing. The miners were giving up and leaving. Instead of crying about misfortune, Greaves simply turned the herd loose at Walachin on the Thompson River. It looked as though the cattle business had come to an end, at least for awhile, and Greaves went on to Soda Creek where he worked as a butcher for the next three years.

"What can be as useless as a critter you can't sell and can't eat?" people were asking when Greaves went back to the Thompson River range to round up and count his cattle. The herd had grown greatly and he branded calves, yearlings and two-year-olds he had never seen before. Moreover, the cattle were fat, and opportunities in raising stock right there captured his interest. Often in the next few years he would cut out a small herd of fat steers and drive to Yale or all the way to New Westminster, one difficult mile after another. But the trails held no terrors for this man who had seen the worst of them.

Occasionally, Victoria's newspaper, the *British Colonist*, would report that Joe Greaves had arrived with cattle. On April 30, 1876, it was: "Mr. Greaves brought down thirty-one head of fat beeves from Cache Creek," and on June 11, 1876: "Mr. Greaves of Cache Creek brought in a band of about twenty head of fine cattle for F. Reynolds, by the Enterprise yesterday. We have seen larger cattle but seldom any in better condition."

⤜⟐⟐⚬⟐⟐⤛

BY 1880, THE CATTLE POPULATION in the Interior had grown far beyond the consuming capacity of little communities anywhere in the province. The situation with respect to surplus stock was even worse than when Thaddeus Harper took the big herd south four years earlier. Wiseacres were still questioning, "What's more useless than a steer nobody needs or wants?"

It was at this point that Greaves, as he presumably told Tom Stewart, resolved to relieve the local stagnation by taking a substantial number of cattle to some place south of the boundary where consuming communities were bigger. In the light of Harper's experience it was a logical proposal and Joseph B. Greaves was a logical person to carry it out.

As Tom Stewart related, the herd assembled for the great expedition comprised four thousand head, many of them belonging to Greaves but not all. Included were big, rough steers with enough rings on their horns to make them seven or eight years old and some were almost as wild as the inter-mountain moose with which they had shared the ranges. With twenty or more riders, the huge mass of cattle was guided, ever so slowly, from Kamloops to the Okanagan Trail and south through the States of Washington and Oregon. Greaves knew the country, knew the pitfalls, knew the necessity of driving according to a plan. The cattle reached the southern border of Oregon at the end of summer and as soon as snow fell, they were turned eastward and driven over the dry country which would not have afforded drinking water at any other season.

Nobody suggested that the Greaves cattle were driven to Chicago, rather that they were pressed eastward to Cheyenne in the southeast corner of Wyoming. To that point the Union Pacific Railway had penetrated in 1867 and almost a year after the cowboys rode out of Kamloops, they loaded their cattle on freight cars and saw them hauled away toward Chicago. Greaves went along and saw the big city, saw his cattle sold.

The undertaking, in Greaves' opinion, was a success. He could report, again according to Tom Stewart, that losses along the way were no greater than they would be in a big herd kept on a home range. His one regret was that he had not taken an additional three months to complete the trip and in that way reached Chicago at a time when cattle prices were stronger.

Greaves returned to British Columbia with added enthusiasm, surer than ever that the proposed railroad coupled with bigger human population would create markets for inter-mountain cattle. Already the CPR rails were laid as far as Brandon and with the drive of William Van Horne were being extended steadily. Once construction was started in the mountains there would be hundreds of additional construction men to be fed. Clearly there would be an advantage in buying up cattle, and Greaves sensed it. One trouble: it would take a lot of capital.

>─┤◄►─•─O─•─◄►┤─◄

IN JANUARY, 1882, GREAVES AND FIVE OTHERS—Peter O'Reilly, J. D. Pemberton, Ben Van Volkenburg, C. W. R. Thomson and W. C. Ward—formed a syndicate to deal in cattle. In the autumn of the next year, Greaves was in a separate partnership with C. M. Beak, thereby gaining an interest in the land held formerly by Thomas Douglas whose name was given to Douglas Lake. Then, with some members of the Syndicate dropping out, a new partnership resulted with Greaves, Beak, Ward and Thomson in it and in 1886, this group became incorporated as the Douglas Lake Cattle Company.

Greaves had been buying cattle extensively and the new company faced its first winter with a big inventory. As misfortune would have it, however, the winter turned out to be the most wicked in human memory. The snow was deep and the cold intense. In the words of one who felt its blasts: "The rabbits froze in mid air and in the spring we still had snow when we should have had flowers."

Douglas Lake losses ran into thousands of head. With such reverses at the beginning of company operations, it might have been accepted as a signal to stop; but Greaves, showing no loss of determination, began at once to rebuild the depleted herd. In the years following, twenty thousand head were sometimes on the ranch, and the person who had come to the continent as a stowaway, friendless and penniless, continued to direct the huge operations there in the Nicola Valley until his 80th year.

Until his death at Victoria in 1915, a few days before his 84th birthday, Joseph Blackbourne Greaves, his eyes bright and face resembling that of King Edward VII, was still the acknowledged leader in his chosen industry.

Christianity and Cows

>━┤━◀▸━●━◂▸━┤━◁

"CHRISTIANITY AND COWS!" said Reverend John McDougall, pioneer Methodist missionary who saw Fort Edmonton in 1862, "that's what they need in this far West."

Unstintingly he gave of his energy to bring both to the land of Indians, traders and buffalo. His was the distinction of having taken the first breeding cattle from Red River to what is now Central Alberta and, later, the first to the Valley of the Bow River where ranching was to flourish. Neither undertaking in the '60s and '70s of last century was easy.

In 1860 the McDougall family followed husband and father, Rev. George McDougall, from Owen Sound, Ontario, to a mission field at Norway House and couple of years later when the missionary was about to embark upon an inspection tour as far west as Fort Edmonton, nineteen-year-old John volunteered to go along to guide the ecclesiastical canoe. Captivated by the primitive country far up the Saskatchewan River, the young fellow resolved to remain and follow his father's example, pursuing missionary work for the church.

>━┤━◀▸━●━◂▸━┤━◁

THERE WAS NO EVIDENCE of farming anywhere except at Fort Edmonton, where a plot of thirty acres on the river flat was being cultivated indifferently. As when Captain John Palliser was there a couple of years before, the one hundred and fifty people living in and about the Hudson's Bay Company post depended almost entirely upon the buffalo for food. Two buffalo carcasses a day were average consumption, testifying to robust and uninhibited appetites. And as for breeding cattle, one may presume that the only specimens in Rupert's Land west of Red River were at Fort Pelly where Palliser mentioned seeing them on the Hudson's Bay Company farm.

Ox-drawn carts had penetrated as far as Fort Edmonton, hence the bovine shape was not entirely strange to the people living there, but John McDougall, with a prophet's vision of farming on that rich soil, resolved to bring cattle for milking and breeding.

He was a thousand miles from Fort Garry—that far from all supplies except buffalo meat—and when, in 1864, it was necessary to go to that place, he chose travel by trail rather than by river.

After a two month's journey by horse and cart—about the usual time for an overland trip—John McDougall was at Fort Garry making the necessary purchases—cattle and other things—to be taken back across the endless buffalo range to his mission at Victoria, ninety miles northeast of Fort Edmonton.

What did he buy? Four cows and a bull costing from $15 to $18 each; oxen, "fine big fellows" at $35 each; "a promising colt, descendant of Fireaway," for $70; three dogs at no recorded price, and ten sacks of flour at $8. These were the essentials, the chief reasons for making the long and trying journey.

For the return, John McDougall's party included a total of five men, among them a stranger going to the mountains and wise enough to avoid travelling alone. On the first day of July they took their departure, but didn't make much progress because of trouble keeping the cattle on the trail. The animals couldn't be blamed for wanting to go back because home has its own fascination even for a cow. The red bull shook his long head defiantly but was no more troublesome than his female companions. One cow in particular was determined to return to her shelter at the settlement.

Christian patience was tested and, finally, McDougall haltered her and tied her to the back of a cart drawn by the heaviest ox. Still the cow rebelled and threw herself when the rope tightened. But the powerful ox plodded on, dragging her across a stone-strewn creek bed, presumably rattling some of the stubbornness out of her. At the end of that ordeal she elected to walk more peacefully.

>─┤◆├─○─┤◆├─<

AFTER THE FIRST WEEK, the cattle, like Abraham going into a far country, seemed to learn exactly what was expected of them. "Let one of those ironless carts squeak," wrote John McDougall, "and the cows were up and alongside with all the alacrity of a soldier answering the bugle note."

The conditions of travel were not good. It rained nearly every day for the first three weeks in July, making trails soft and heavy. And there being no tent in the party, the men slept under their carts where they were exposed to the mosquitoes coming in swarms to gorge upon human blood. For the benefit of the cattle, smudges were made each night.

There were rivers to cross, rivers without bridges. At the swollen White Mud running into Lake Manitoba, cart wheels were removed and lashed together to make a raft for the crossing. The Little Saskatchewan was running less boisterously and could be forded without difficulty. As carts and cattle skirted the shore of Shoal Lake, however, there was another aquatic experience. The "promising colt" bought at Fort Garry was a three-year-old filly, not yet broken. An additional riding horse would be an advantage in driving the cattle and chasing buffalo. Here, thought John McDougall, might be an easy way of breaking a horse to ride. Removing his clothing, he went out in the lake, leading the haltered filly, somewhat against her will.

When the water was deep enough for swimming, McDougall slipped onto the mare's back. In her surprise, she plunged a few times but quickly discovered she couldn't swim and fight at the same time. To swim was necessary for survival.

But nearer shore, with feet again on firm bottom, the mare exercised her right to buck. McDougall promptly headed her back into deeper water and in an extremely short time, all thought of resisting was forgotten. That afternoon, he rode the mare on the trail. Her behaviour was excellent.

Evidently the Assiniboine in its broad, green valley was in flood because it took two days to raft the freight across. Then there was a delay when one of the cows disappeared—just strayed away to find shelter from bulldog flies in a thick grove of trees.

The next excitement was when McDougall and his charges were camping for a night in the Touchwood Hills. They were one month out from Fort Garry and roughly half way to Fort Edmonton. During the hours of darkness, McDougall was awakened by the barking of his dogs. He sat up, reached for his gun and remained motionless to listen for any unusual sounds. In a moment the shadowy figure of an Indian was visible in the moonlight, crawling toward the camp, no doubt with the intention of stealing the precious cows or horses or taking some white scalps. Obviously, there was an evil purpose and only one way by which to deal with such a situation. Aiming in the general direction of the figure he fired. In the stillness of the Touchwood Hills night it sounded like the roar of a Fort Garry cannon. Horses and cattle jumped nervously and sleeping men bounded to their feet. The figure in the grass leaped into the air, evidently hit by the bullet. It was unfortunate but what else could a man of peace do in the face of certain violence? As soon as daylight returned, a search was conducted but there was no trace of the Indian and it was concluded that, at least, he wasn't killed.

>-+-◆>-+-O-+-◆+-+-<

DAYS LATER THERE WAS THE SOUTH SASKATCHEWAN RIVER to cross and it proved almost too much for the men. Saskatoon didn't exist but the party came to the river a few miles north of where that city had its birth about eighteen years later.

The river was high from prolonged rains and the travellers reached it on a Saturday evening. All day Sunday, while cattle grazed and ruminated, the men watched deadfall trees racing by on the swollen current, and wondered how they were to cope with a crossing.

In the willows beside the water they found a skin canoe, evidently left by Hudson's Bay Company men, and on Monday morning the shapeless thing was pressed into service, taking freight across at the rate of four hundred pounds each trip. It was tricky. The canoe made of leather was like a body without bones and the current being strong, the thing was carried far down at each crossing. The haul upstream along the shore was greater than the distance across but by sundown, with patience and good luck, flour and other inert freight were securely piled on the far side. There remained the horses, cattle and carts and nobody was sure how Fort Garry milk cows and an unprincipled red bull would respond to the necessity of a long swim.

For Tuesday morning's operations, the carts were assembled into one big raft, with wheels tied on the underside. To guide this invention in the water, a long rope was attached and held by a man going ahead in the canoe. The principle was fair enough but it was much like a tugboat hauling a boom of logs on a stormy sea and in mid-stream the rope broke. For one dark moment the men saw themselves stranded, four hundred miles from home, while carts floated toward Lake Winnipeg.

Fortunately, the man in the canoe had the presence of mind to pursue, and some distance down he overtook the raft and picked up the short end of the broken rope. With difficulty he succeeded in easing the load to the west bank and mooring it in the mud. It was far below the point at which the freight was piled but it was good to know that the carts were now secure and on the proper side.

There were still the cattle to be forced over. Brought to water's edge, they were coaxed, then pressed to enter but with the best of bovine sagacity, they were afraid of the great expanse of fast water and refused to leave dry ground. Again, McDougall resorted to the skin canoe and rope. One cow, with rope about her neck, was forced into the water and convinced against her will that she had to follow the canoe. The other cattle, chased by yelling men to the water's edge, impulsively followed. Once in the stream they accepted the necessity of the long swim and made better time than the canoe. Once or twice in the middle of the river, the cows appeared to be in trouble but as often as one was carried out of sight, she re-appeared and, finally, all members of the little herd, the red bull at the lead, walked out on the opposite shore, exhausted but safe.

The canoe made one more return crossing to bring the other men and late on Tuesday everything was safely lodged on the west side, ready for the drive to Fort Carlton where the even bigger North Saskatchewan would have to be crossed. But at Carlton, McDougall borrowed a better boat and the crossing was made in comparatively good time.

The biggest road obstacles were now behind but there were still Indians with uncertain temper and the danger of cattle being swept away by mighty herds of buffalo. But each succeeding week-day found the McDougall party eighteen or twenty miles nearer destination. At Fort Pitt, Reverend George McDougall met his son, admired the cattle, and accompanied them for the remainder of the journey to Victoria.

>─┤─◆─○─◆┤─<

AND SO, AFTER FIFTY-SIX TRAVELLING DAYS from Fort Garry, John McDougall and his carts and cattle were at journey's end. It was good to be home; it was also good to have a herd of milk cows, first in that part. On the trail, McDougall wrote, "the cows were a great source of comfort to our party; they assured us of milk and butter and if other resources failed, of beef also." Now they would furnish the same diversified comfort at the mission. Indians came to gaze at them. Trappers came to admire.

Like true pioneers, the four cows and one bull recognized their responsibilities and went to work making dairy products where none had been known before, reproducing their kind where no domestic calves were dropped before. None the

worse for the thousand-mile journey and dangerous river crossings, the herd inspired further interest in domestic livestock.
Surely these, the first domestic cattle in an area now well known
for its mixed farming, deserve a place of honor on the pages of
agricultural history.

First in the Bow Valley

JOHN MCDOUGALL'S METHODIST COWS driven full length of the thousand-mile trail from Fort Garry to the mission northeast of Fort Edmonton in 1864, dropped calves with all the regularity of robins returning annually to nest in the North. The sulky red bull which had been exposed to recitation of scripture day after day on the same long trail, saw his offspring growing in numbers and growing in fatness on grass where only buffalo grazed before. But for these mission-sheltered cattle there were yet other far frontiers; when Reverend John and Trader David McDougall decided to make their homes among Stoney Indians in the foothills west of where Fort Calgary would be built, they were able to draw upon their own herd for breeding stock they proposed to take.

The drive from Edmonton to the place beside the Bow River, later called Morley, was not a long one like the trail from Fort Garry but it was important inasmuch as the breeding cattle concerned were the first of their kind in what came to be regarded by many stockmen as the best ranching country in the West—by a few as best in the world. Ox teams from Fort Benton, Montana, probably preceded them into what is now Southern Alberta, but McDougall's were the first breeding cattle.

BY THIS TIME, THE MISSIONARY MCDOUGALL knew the plains like a river pilot knows his channel. He had travelled extensively, hunted buffalo with the Cree, and visited the Indians wherever he could find them. He knew also that adventures south into the country of Blackfoot and tribal allies were considered dangerous. Whisky traders from the South were going into the valleys of Oldman, Belly, Highwood and Bow rivers but fur traders preferred to conduct with less hostile customers.

Notwithstanding the added risks, it was the missionary's conviction that he could do the greatest service by locating among the Stoney and, in 1873, he was moving with his family and taking along a foundation of twelve cattle—eleven cows and one bull—all descended directly from the Fort Garry stock.

Horses, carts and cattle were ready for departure from Fort Edmonton at the end of October. The cavalcade would be impressive—twenty-nine Red River carts and wagons loaded with supplies and equipment, saddle horses and loose horses and cattle. Accompanying would be Mrs. John McDougall, the missionary's eldest daughter Flora, his brother David and a score or more of half-breed helpers. Altogether, thirty-five persons were making the trip, some for no other reason than the adventure. "Our only proviso," wrote Reverend John, in referring to the people who sought to join the party, "was no whisky or firewater in any shape."

Having assembled close to the Hudson's Bay Company post, the expedition's first serious test was making the crossing on the North Saskatchewan River. Being low at that season of the year, the river could be forded but ice was forming and the necessity of taking to the water was cold and uninviting. Horses balked at first and cattle entered only after a lot of maneuvering and prodding on the part of the men.

Emerging on the south side, thoroughly chilled, cattle and horses shook icy water from their hides and looked back wistfully at the familiar Fort Edmonton setting on the other side.

Now, however, there was a trail, one of Indian making, to guide the party and with the least delay the ox-drawn and horse-drawn carts were brought into tandem positions to form a "train," the reliable helper known as Donald taking the lead. Mrs. John McDougall was driving a wagon and Miss Flora, with a little girl's love for riding, was on her saddle horse and undertaking to keep the loose cattle and horses moving on or beside the trail. The McDougall men, well mounted, well armed and acting as outriders, helped wherever needed.

Because of their wet hides, the cattle wanted to run and Flora needed assistance for the first few miles. Then, as the stock became easier to guide, the McDougall men, fully conscious of dangers in that section, rode far ahead as scouts, or well behind as rear guards.

>─┤─◆>─○─<◆─┤─<

INDIAN SUMMER WAS GONE; rabbits were changing color and there were other reminders of winter. The hope was to reach Bow River before snowfall made it difficult or impossible to use carts. Days were becoming shorter. The travellers pressed forward until sundown and camped for the first night at a place marked later by oil-famous Leduc. On the second night—a Saturday night—they were at the Peace Hills, known to Indians as Wetuskewin, where hunting parties of Cree and Blackfoot once had a surprise meeting and made the rare choice of peace instead of slaughter. There the McDougall party remained over Sunday. No wheels turned on that day; instead, men and women assembled for a chilly outdoor service of worship conducted by Reverend John. While cattle and horses grazed unattended, the words and notes of Methodist hymns rose Heavenward on lusty voices. There was dignity befitting a fine church and the minister preached and prayed with the stamina of a marathoner.

Perhaps it was the echo of raucous singing that brought puzzled Indians to the white man's camp. But there was no reason for alarm; they were friendly Cree led by John McDougall's "old friend, Muddy Bull ... among the salt of the earth."

There was frost in the air and an icy crispness in the old grass when cattle were gathered and carts made ready to resume the journey on Monday morning. Three days later the travellers forded the Red Deer River. It was thought to be the half-way mark and John McDougall announced a halt in the hope of replenishing meat supplies. The country along the Red Deer was known to be good for buffalo.

While carts remained stationary, the two McDougall men and other experienced hunters rode east and south. Having traded horses that day, John McDougall was especially anxious to try his new thoroughbred mare called Favorite, one which David McDougall brought originally from Fort Garry. The mare had speed and when the hunters encountered a herd of about forty buffalo bulls, the mare brought her rider in fast and John shot the first bull. More buffalo fell and the balance of the day was spent in conveying meat to the camp.

Cart-train travel resumed, cattle and loose horses now walking along co-operatively and Miss Flora guiding them like a seasoned cowboy. It was pleasant country—big country.

At night, camp was made close to where the town of Innisfail stands today. All was peaceful when men and women made their beds on the frozen ground but during the hours of darkness, suddenly, there was the noise of galloping feet. Men springing from their beds supposed, quite naturally, that Indians were driving the horses away in a grand robbery. In the black of night it was impossible to see exactly what had happened, except that the horses and cattle were gone—not even a saddle horse remaining on which a man might pursue. Until daylight, nothing could be done and, back in their blankets for the balance of the night, sleepless men pondered frustrating thoughts of being stranded one hundred and twenty-five miles from Fort Edmonton with carts and no stock by which to haul them. Almost as serious, the breeding cattle intended as seed stock in a completely new area were gone.

>-+◆>-○-◆+-<

AS SOON AS DAYLIGHT PERMITTED, men carrying guns set out in pursuit. Marks in the frosted grass made it easy to detect the direction of the stampede but tracks seemed strangely numerous. Soon the truth about the disappearance of cattle and horses dawned upon the men. Indians had been suspected unjustly in this instance. Fact was that the domestic animals had been caught in the current of a migrating herd of buffalo and swept away. It could happen and did happen. The question now was: how far would the horses and cattle go with the wild herd?

Fortunately, the domestic stock fell behind as the buffalo continued eastward and the McDougall men overtook their animals after walking for a few miles. A count showed all were there—none missing—and it was simple enough to catch a quiet horse and with it herd the balance of the stock back to camp.

The trail journey resumed but that troubled night's enforced association of buffalo and cattle led to further delay on the morning following. When Flora McDougall rounded up the little herd for the day's march, the bull, son of the old red one from Fort Garry, was missing. It seemed unlikely that the animal was stolen. Indians would not take the bull and leave the horses. Again a search was undertaken with the thought the animal might have sought the shelter of a nearby bluff. That bull's possible importance to the future of cattle breeding in the Bow Valley was not being overlooked. "We must find him," John McDougall said.

When it was evident that nearby groves were not hiding the bull, searchers on horses went farther afield. The day was almost spent when John McDougall spotted a small band of buffalo and pursued with the idea of getting a shot at one. When the herd began to run, one animal lagged behind and at once McDougall recognized his delinquent herd header, lame, bruised, bleeding and unrepentant, trying gamely to keep up with the wild company he had so unwisely chosen.

>─┤◆├─○─┤◆├─<

JOHN MCDOUGALL FORGOT ABOUT SHOOTING A BUFFALO. The domestic bull held his attention. Without difficulty, men were able to turn the disabled warrior and start toward the camp. What had happened was pretty obvious. After the run with buffalo on the previous night, the masculine fellow craved more of the same untamed companionship. During the night he strayed from the domestic herd and forced himself upon the first group of buffalo he encountered. But the reception was anything but cordial. A savage fight had ensued and the wild adversary with more strength and sharper horns was altogether too much for the one handicapped by domestication. The bull from Fort Edmonton was properly beaten but not to the point where he couldn't recover.

As darkness was settling upon the countryside, men rode into camp driving the prodigal bull and making uncomplimentary remarks about his judgment.

Carts and cattle made good progress for two days and then a snow storm kept the travellers in camp for another two. But they were now near journey's end. They were in the foothills, well favored with soil and water. Crossing the "Dog Pond"—Dogpound on modern maps—the party came face to face with Stoney Indians, Chief Bear's Paw among them. Having met the Chief previously and received his approval for the idea of living with his people, John McDougall was received cordially. Next day, Indians guided the party to the mouth of the Ghost River in the Valley of the Bow. Within a day or two a site for building was being fixed upon. Busy days followed; even Sunday was fully occupied, "preaching, singing, praying, baptizing, marrying, answering questions and teaching these eager people as we were able."

For much of the ensuing winter, the cattle—of no particular breeding but hardy—were able to graze out on the hills. The experiment was convincing and next summer, when David McDougall was returning from Fort Benton, whence he went for supplies, he was driving eight more cattle to augment the first herd in the south country. And late in 1875 there was still a bigger development in cattle, seven hundred head brought from the Columbia Lakes by a John Shaw who, on John McDougall's invitation, wintered in the Bow Valley. But the two McDougall brands, JM and O deserve to be regarded as the oldest in southern Alberta.

The Unpopular Police Cattle

THERE IT WAS, THE PRAIRIE SPECTACLE OF THE CENTURY, yet
nobody to capture the scene in picture and only a handful of
humans to even witness it. With Commissioner G. A. French
and Assistant Commissioner James F. Macleod riding in splen-
dor at the front of the long column, the untried force of
Northwest Mounted Police drew away from Fort Dufferin, less
than ten miles inside Manitoba's southern boundary. The
objective was some undetermined part far to the West where
gangster whiskey pedlars freighting from Fort Benton,
Montana, were trading arrogantly and living lawlessly.

In appropriately glowing terms the world heard about the
gallant young men and their pathetically exhausted horses making that westward trek but how many students of western story
are familiar with the cattle and oxen taken on the same historic
expedition? The purpose in taking cattle was two-fold; they
would be something for hungry policemen to fall back upon if
rations of buffalo meat failed, and the idea of stocking a police
farm with breeding animals was thought by some of the government's advisers to be practical. But the sense of need for cattle was not shared by men in uniform; the herd, in simple fact,
was unpopular.

A SHAMEFUL MASSACRE in the Cypress Hills a year earlier, coupled with reports about ruthless trading in fire-water, had convinced the Canadian government of the urgent need for law enforcement and by Act of Parliament, in 1873, the force was authorized. Recruiting and planning began at once and on June 6, 1874, a special train left Toronto carrying sixteen officers, two hundred and one young men, and two hundred and forty-four horses. There being no rails in the Canadian West, the Mounties could go only as far as Fargo, North Dakota, by train; from there to Dufferin there was nothing better than a poor cart trail. At the latter point the men from the East were joined by Colonel Macleod and a smaller group of police recruits which had wintered at Fort Garry.

Suddenly, the hitherto obscure post known as Dufferin became a centre of intense activity as supplies were assembled and men prepared for a long and perilous march.

Notwithstanding the absence of spectators—except for a few bewildered and unsympathetic Natives—there was order and grandeur and color in the formation. Moreover, here was magnitude; in addition to the rookie policemen there were three hundred and eight horses, one hundred and forty-two oxen, one hundred and fourteen Red River carts, seventy-three wagons, twenty Metis drivers, implements like mowing machines and the ninety-three other cattle whose disorderly movements made them quite objectionable to the men of military bearing. Strung out in marching order, the cavalcade extended for two full miles along the trail—about as long as a Calgary Stampede parade.

Buffalo country, far from human settlement, was not where one would expect parade order even to the point of matching colors in the horses. In the absence of public gaze it might have been thought of no consequence if men slouched in their saddles or grey horses teamed with chestnuts. But leaders with strong views about discipline figured it did matter and, except for cows and calves insisting upon breaking ranks, it was a parade all the way.

The column, its "sweetness" wasted "on the desert air," was described in the Commissioner's initial report: "First came A Division with splendid dark bays and thirteen wagons. Then B with dark browns. Next C with bright chestnuts drawing the guns and ammunition. Next, D with greys, then E with black horses, the rear being brought up by F with light bays. Then a motley string of ox carts, ox wagons, cattle for slaughter, cows, calves, mowing machines, etc."

And to think that, apart from a few Natives, no spectators were present to witness.

"To a stranger," the Commissioner added, "it would have appeared an astonishing cavalcade; armed men and guns looked as if fighting was to be done. What could ploughs, harrows, mowing machines, cows, calves, etc., be for? But that little force had a double duty to perform: to fight if necessary but, in any case, to establish posts in the far West."

⊱―◈―○―◈―⊰

THERE WAS HARDSHIP FROM THE BEGINNING. Before Pembina Mountain came in sight, it was perfectly plain that the loads were too heavy for the horses and oxen; and watering places were often far apart. Commissioner French may have recalled a warning he heard before leaving Dufferin, that horses lost would probably run to sixty percent.

The oxen survived the demands better than the horses which needed more oats than supplies allowed. To make matters worse for the horses, the eastern horsemen, unfamiliar with prairie forage, forced their animals to feed upon the tall slough grass with nutritional quality far inferior to that of the short upland kinds.

At Roche Percee, two hundred and seventy miles from the starting point, the Commissioners called for a rest period—and well they might. Already three horses were dead and three others abandoned when they could continue no longer. With so many of the poor brutes near the point of exhaustion, a change of plans seemed necessary. It was now Commissioner French's conclusion that the contingent was too big and cumbersome; his resolve was to divide it, send Inspector W. D. Jarvis and A Troop with the less essential stock to Fort Ellice and, perhaps, Fort Edmonton.

"Jarvis," wrote French in his diary, "takes fifty-five horses, twenty-four wagons, fifty-five carts, sixty-two oxen and fifty cows with calves." The horses cut out for the more northerly trip were the ones considered too weak to continue with the main party, and the cattle were all sent except ten head which French evidently felt duty-bound to retain.

Clearly, the cattle had lost none of their unpopularity with Mounties of all ranks. They were unglamorous; they were impediments to progress on the trail. But planners who ordered cannons to be lugged across the plains believed cattle also should go. So, go they must—somewhere. There was a small number of breeding cattle at Fort Edmonton at this time but none in the southwest where the police hoped to build a post.

Now, after a few days of rest, the main part of the cattle herd was being driven northward in the direction of Moose Mountain and on to Fort Ellice—perhaps on to Edmonton—partly because Commissioner French considered it a handicap. Sick men drove the wagons for Jarvis and able ones drove the cattle. Generally, the mid-summer countryside was peaceful. Once, Sioux Indians with expressions betraying their hatred appeared but the police made a pretense of ignoring them and rode on without incident.

Worrying Jarvis more than Indians was the fact of not knowing what he would do with the cattle. Nobody at Fort Ellice, Fort Pelly, or Fort Edmonton said they wanted more cattle, and if Inspector Jarvis could have quietly lost his bovine charges or shot them into outer space without leaving a trace, no doubt he'd have done it gladly. He was a policeman—not a cattleman—and if the people at Fort Ellice would accept all or any part of the tired and footsore herd, he would ride on toward Edmonton with a feeling of relief.

BUT AT FORT ELLICE on August 12, he found no enthusiasm for a big herd—nearly a hundred head. There was neither feed nor winter quarters for so many. But anxious to see less of these animals which added nothing to the appearance of a mounted troop, Jarvis agreed to a proposal to divert most of them to Fort Pelly or Fort Livingstone where at least a few cattle were being kept already.

Leaving behind about two-thirds of the cattle to be driven over the one hundred mile trail to Fort Pelly, Jarvis took the Carlton-Edmonton Trail to the west with just fifteen cows, fourteen calves and one bull.

In due course the cattle left behind arrived at Fort Pelly where the Hudson's Bay Company had a farm but they were not wanted and pretty soon travel was resumed toward Fort Livingstone where a Mounted Police post was under construction. But at this new post beside the Swan River, a feed shortage made the reception even colder.

Meanwhile, the main force under Col. Macleod was nearing the foothills, having staged a triumphant attack on defenceless Fort Whoop-Up. Finally, beside the Oldman River where Fort Macleod was to be built, the Assistant Commissioner figured the police had come seven hundred and eighty-one miles, "and after the first eighteen [miles] had not seen a single human habitation except a few Indian wigwams."

Many of the horses were dead and men weary. Only the little group of ten cattle herded behind the cavalcade seemed to have no ill effects. But having reached journey's end, and winter coming on, Colonel Macleod had to decide what to do with these and other animals not immediately needed. The problem may have worried him but on October 27, he reported: "I have come to the conclusion to send sixty-four horses and twenty oxen with the ten young cattle to winter at Sun River." That would mean a further trip of two hundred miles and Inspector Walsh and thirteen men of the force—including the immortal guide and scout Jerry Potts—were assigned the task of driving the mixed herd. It was arranged, also, that Constable Cochrane of B Troop would remain in Montana to watch the stock during the winter months.

The truth was that neither the Assistant Commissioner nor anybody else in authority had the slightest confidence that livestock could be wintered on the broad range which is now southern Alberta. Reverend John McDougall had wintered a small herd of cattle beside the Bow River near Morley in the previous season but two years were to elapse before anybody would perform the outdoor experiment at Fort Macleod.

Jarvis, on the long trip to Fort Edmonton with the thirty loose cattle in his care, found the trials of the trail no less numerous. At Fort Carlton the carts were ferried across the broad North Saskatchewan and the unwilling cattle were forced to swim. And not only did Jarvis lose horses from exhaustion but in a period of eight days he was obliged to record one calf and two oxen dead, and four oxen abandoned. The day after abandoning three of the played-out oxen, he and his troop arrived at Victoria, fifty miles northeast of Fort Edmonton. There he was happy to make a deal whereby eleven oxen and all the cows and calves would be left for the winter. Relieved, he rode on to Fort Edmonton, completing a journey of close to nine hundred miles from Roche Percee, eleven hundred miles from Dufferin, and with the company of cattle nearly all the way.

><->-O-<->-<

COMMISSIONER FRENCH, in the meantime, had turned back to make his way to the new Swan River post called Livingstone. There he received bad news: fire had destroyed more than half the hay in stacks, leaving enough winter feed for the horses but little for cattle. Next day, riding toward Fort Pelly, he "met a drove of eighty-four cattle enroute to Swan River and turned them back," instructing that the herd be taken again to Fort Ellice where there was a slightly better chance of finding winter feed.

Truly, the cattle which were unfortunate enough to have been acquired for Mounted Police purposes were being shifted "from pillar to post." Perhaps no herd in Canadian history cost so much time and trouble. The hapless cattle, numbering about a hundred when leaving Dufferin on July 8, were now five months later, scattered at points more than a thousand miles apart. Apart from the oxen, ten head were wintering deep in Montana; about thirty head were at Victoria and the remainder at Fort Ellice.

Tom Lynch on the
Longhorn Trail

FOR VOLUME OF TRAIL DUST consumed or inhaled, beady-eyed Tom Lynch who would accept any cattle driving assignment—anywhere—could surely qualify for the Canadian record. He, more than any other, was responsible for extending the trail over which the Texas breed of cattle penetrated to Canadian ranges. United States "Highway 91" and Alberta's "Number 4" leading to Lethbridge and Fort Macleod, marking the general route for herd after herd brought to stock the northern ranches, might very properly have been called the Tom Lynch Trail.

And no less worthy of ranchland immortality was his partner on the earliest trailing expeditions, big-bodied and fatherly George Emerson. Throughout the latter parts of their lives, both men could claim High River. It was where they chose to live and die. There Emerson was buried but for Lynch whose passing occurred in 1892, burial had to be at Calgary because the flourishing community beside the Highwood, scarcely conscious of illness, old age or death, had not yet provided such convenience as a cemetery.

Missouri-born and Montana-raised Tom Lynch, perfectly at ease in handling mules, horses and bandits, blended beautifully with the general character of High River. Nothing short of a horse race could excite him. While still in his teens he was riding with trail-hardened cow-hands taking Oregon cattle to min-ing camps in western Montana. He took to the saddle like a pup to a greasy bone and, with a boy's curiosity, crossed the Canadian border and rode as far as Fort Edmonton where he found George Emerson panning for gold on the North Saskatchewan.

At that time neither Lynch nor Emerson had any thoughts of ranching. But riding together back to Montana they sensed a probable increase in human activity there-about and agreed that sooner or later somebody would make a tidy profit by driving southern cattle into the Northwest Territories and selling them.

"Take this Fort Macleod place," Lynch said with a sweep of his roping arm, "a lot of police there—paying 75 cents a pound for their butter—and short of meat. No cattle except about six milk cows divided between Henry Olson and Joe McFarland. We better chase some in here next spring and sell 'em. What you say to that?"

>─┼─◆─○─◆─┼─◄

CAME THE SPRING OF 1877 and Lynch and Emerson did return with a small herd of Montana cattle. The animals sold readily enough to Ed Maunsell and other members of the Mounted Police who were taking early discharge by providing substitutes to finish out their required terms. Several of those choosing early graduation from the police ranks were cautiously consid-ering ranching nearby, having been impressed by the enforced but none the less important ranchland experiment in the pre-ceding months. It was like this: late in the autumn of 1876, John B. Smith of Sun River, Montana, had driven fourteen cows, ten calves and one bull to Fort Macleod for the purpose of selling them. Somehow, the herd was acquired by Mounted Police Constable Whitney (Reg. No. 102). Observers supposed Whitney bought the cattle. But why would he? Why would a police officer with full-time occupation and subject to military discipline be buying cattle and thus dividing his attention?

The more plausible explanation is that Whitney didn't buy the herd but, rather, won it in a quiet poker game and then

wondered what he would or could do with it. He had neither
shelter nor winter feed for cattle and, accepting the inevitabil-
ity of loss, he turned the animals loose to rustle for the winter.

"You'll never see those critters again," Whitney was told. "If
they don't die from freezing, you can expect the Blood Indians
to shoot them down—or the buffalo to sweep them away. Could
be they'll end up in Wyoming. Good thing they didn't cost you
anything. You'll never see hide or hair of 'em again."

Whitney was conscious of all the dangers; he knew about the
recent Custer Massacre and that the Indians were in a bad mood.
He knew all about the enormous buffalo herds. But in commit-
ting the cattle to the harshness of a North Western winter, he had
no alternative. Out they went and, temporarily, he managed to
forget about them. He had other duties and wasn't supposed to
be in the cattle business anyway. But when spring came again,
Whitney's curiosity took him on a search for some trace of the
cattle, dead or alive. After an absence of a couple of days, he rode
back to Fort Macleod, driving the entire herd of twenty-five cattle—and every cow had a new calf. It looked as though it might
be the beginning of Prairie ranching on the Canadian side
although young Mounties taking early discharge were still fear-
ful that Whitney's experience stemmed only from good luck.

ONE OF THOSE PREPARED to repeat the test in the fall of 1877 was
Fred Kanouse, reformed whisky trader searching for some
legitimate occupation. Coming from Fort Benton, he had seen
the Canadian grass for the first time in 1871. Now, while
Blackfoot Treaty Number Seven was being signed at Blackfoot
Crossing on the Bow, Kanouse was driving twenty-one cows
and a bull from the Missouri River and turning them loose at
Fort Macleod about as nonchalantly as an ox chews cud. Next
spring Kanouse conducted a one-man round-up with precisely
the same result as that experienced by Whitney.

It was convincing. Lynch and Emerson may have heard
about it. In any case, before the buffalo cows were through

calving, the two young fellows were driving north from Musselshell River with nearly one hundred cattle, not sure how far they'd go before finding customers. They came to Fort Macleod but instead of stopping there, they drove right on another three hundred miles to Fort Edmonton and sold to good advantage.

Now while Tom Lynch and George Emerson were riding back to winter quarters, they made one of their most important decisions. "Driving and selling won't always be good," Emerson told his partner. "Maybe we should be thinking about starting our own ranch somewhere. How'd it be to run cows up in this country. Look at that grass beside the Highwood River. I never in all my days saw the beat of it—and but a few buffalo eating it. What do you think about getting our own brand and keeping the next bunch right here beside the river—see if there's any future in cattle up here?"

Tom Lynch, who had been entertaining the same thoughts, rode west along the Highwood, studied the grass, kicked up some soil to see its color, and picked out a good site for a cow-camp beside the old Spitzie Trading Post, then returned to the Crossing to tell George Emerson he was in favor of bringing in a herd for themselves. "Can't think of a better place," he repeated.

And so, early in 1879, one of the most significant herds of the period was being assembled at Miles City for a long drive to the North and West. The herd contained a thousand cattle—biggest group to cross the International Boundary up to that time.

In a very real sense the trail by way of Bear's Paw Mountains, Sweetgrass Hills and iniquitous Fort Whoop-Up, over which the cattle were travelling, was the first extension of the greater one originating in Texas right after the Civil War and pounded by millions of bovine feet. Between 1873 and 1887 when grass began to grow again on the trails, not fewer than seven million southern cattle were driven to Dodge City, Kansas, alone.

AT FIRST, THE CATTLE FROM THE SOUTH were intended for slaughter only but gradually, as buffalo disappeared, there was interest in stocking the Colorado, Wyoming, and Montana grass. In the summer of 1879, close to a quarter of a million southern cattle were delivered to the Montana ranges. The cattle frontier was gradually but surely being pushed northward.

To get the thousand cattle fresh in from the South, Lynch and Emerson had to outbid the Montana men who wanted breeding stock. Like other cattle from the South, these were not far removed in point of time from the longhorn ranges of Texas. Many of the individuals were typical of the lanky, cat-hammed Rio Grande cattle. One of the bulls accompanying the drive was said to be half a hand higher than the horse Tom Lynch usually rode. "Old Yellow" as he was known, had only one horn, the other having been lost in one of many battles for range supremacy. With both horns the spread would have been close to eight feet. But even with one horn, Old Yellow could fight a demon and send younger bulls into retreat.

With long and unbalanced head, sides as flat as stable doors and hook bones resembling hat racks, Old Yellow could outrun all but the best horses. Like others of his kind, he harboured no love for humans and, though generally ready to take the lead in a trail herd, was equally ready to plunge wickedly at man or horse coming too close to him. In conformation and temperament, the longhorn was about everything a modern cattleman does not want but Tom Lynch liked Old Yellow and the bull was on the Canadian range until overtaken by natural death.

It was midsummer when that first big herd was driven past Fort Macleod and north on the Fort Calgary Trail. The grass was taller and the hills more inviting than the men had seen before. One thing was strangely different: the buffalo herds. Three years earlier as Lynch and Emerson rode through the same area, the buffalo were there in millions. Now only a few were to be seen. The slaughter had been on a gigantic scale. Indians receiving insufficient beef were hungry. Complete destruction of what Rev. John McDougall called "God's cattle" seemed certain and not many people were showing concern.

After fording the Highwood River at Spitzie Crossing, the immigrant longhorns were turned toward the glistening mountain peaks and released to graze and multiply on the most generous grass encountered on the long tour.

>──◆──○──◆──<

THE WINTER OF 1879–'80 WAS EARLIER AND COLDER than usual but the new cattle came through well and were still close to the river in the spring. Moreover, Tom Lynch and George Emerson were on the Canadian range to stay. After a while the partnership was dissolved with Emerson going farther west in the hills and Lynch crossing to the south side of the Highwood and using the TL brand. Emerson became a conventional rancher—a good one—but for some years Lynch continued to be a driver of trail herds more than a producer. He brought the first cattle for the North West Cattle Company, the first for the Military Colonization Ranch, the first horses for the Quorn, horses for the High River Horse Ranch and foundation herds for various ranchers at Pincher Creek.

When trailing ceased, Lynch moved farther west also, and located a second TL ranch on the north side of his beloved Highwood. After three years at the upper place, he died suddenly, died in Calgary while attending a court case. He had lived in the High River area only thirteen years but, as nobody would deny, his influence extended far across the Canadian West. Men who knew him remembered him as a skillful horseman, a big-hearted neighbor ready to help anybody in need, and a trail driver without a superior.

The Cochrane Cattle

LYNCH AND EMERSON GAMBLED with the first big herd to range in the Canadian foothills; Senator Mathew Henry Cochrane of Compton, Quebec, gambled with the second and bigger one—three thousand head driven four hundred miles from Central Montana to the Bow River, late in 1881.

Earlier in the year the federal government, finally becoming conscious of grass resources in the West, made provision for twenty-one-year leases on up to 100,000 acres. Rental at one cent an acre per year was reasonable enough but unwise was the stipulation requiring a lessee within three years to stock at least one head of cattle for every ten acres of lease.

It was a time when British capitalists were making big investments in Texas ranches, and Cochrane, with the heart of an explorer, reasoned that the Northwest Territories might offer about as much in opportunity. Already known internationally as a progressive stockman—having imported many of Britain's best Shorthorn, Hereford and Aberdeen-Angus cattle for his Hillhurst Farm in Quebec—Cochrane would now see the western grass for himself.

With buckboard and team of spirited horses bought at Fort Benton, the fifty-seven-year-old Senator drove north over Whoop-Up Trail, studying vegetation each day, sleeping under the stars each night. Grass was turning green and grouse were nesting when he forded the Oldman River and met up with the man who knew more than any other about the country's capabilities. That one was John George "Kootenai" Brown, who had been squatting over against Waterton Lake "since Chief Mountain was just a buffalo-sized rubbing stone."

Brown's proud military bearing was a carry-over from those years in the Queen's Life Guards, terminated, according to story, when he became "too friendly" with certain ladies in the Royal Household and was "shipped" away to India. From India he went to South America and from there trekked north through Mexico and the California gold fields. Certainly he had seen much of the world and was now speaking with authority and some affection about his adopted Foothills and Prairies.

"Damned right!" the scholarly Brown with Oxford accent assured; "this grass is as good as anything in Texas or Montana. Where buffalo liked to feed, cattle will do fine. This'll be good cattle country some day. Damned right!"

>-→--○--←-<

COCHRANE WAS SOON CONVINCED and lost no time in securing a LEASE — 100,000 rolling acres fronting on the crystal-clear Bow River. Next he bought a herd of Montana cattle, three thousand at a price of $16 per head, delivered at the International Boundary. The cattle were considered superior to those brought by Lynch and Emerson; at least most of them were a generation removed from the thinly fleshed longhorns and showed the influence of British breeds on the side of the sires. Not more than a little of their native meanness had been lost but they possessed the added size that accompanies hybrid vigor, and their colors gave hints of Shorthorn, Hereford and Aberdeen-Angus infusions. Indeed, the first breed comparisons in the West were made in the course of the Cochrane drive and one writer noted that animals showing some Aberdeen-Angus characteristics made the trip with the least evidence of hardship.

At once Cochrane faced the necessity of appointing a ranch manager. When stopping at Fort Macleod, he met Major

James Walker of the Mounted Police and invited him to accept the position. Walker was willing but an unexpired term with the force loomed as an obstacle because men of the NWMP did not pack up and leave on any ordinary pretexts. But the driving Conservative Senator believed he could fix things at Ottawa. The problem was carried right to Prime Minister Sir John A. Macdonald and with speed uncommon in government administration, Walker was out of uniform and taking up residence in a new log ranch-house beside Big Hill, awaiting delivery of the cattle.

Escorting the Montana herd to the boundary was Howell Harris, a man well known on the Canadian side, first as a trader and later as a rancher. And then the cattle were turned over to Frank Strong and thirty cowboys employed by I. G. Baker Company whose contract was to take them to meet Walker at the Bow River, the reward to be $2.50 per head.

To make for faster travel, Strong divided the herd into two groups: steers in the advance herd and cows and calves in the second one. But his men were in too much of a hurry and speed proved costly for the Cochrane Company. Sixteen to eighteen miles a day was too fast for steers, leaving little time for grazing, and twelve to fourteen miles a day for cows and calves was no better. Wagons followed the second herd to pick up the calves becoming too tired to continue and when wagons were full, exhausted young animals were abandoned or traded for food or anything offered along the way. A trader with cargo of bootleg whisky, dodging the Mounted Police, exchanged his liquid cargo for enough calves to start him in the cattle business.

The herd arrived at the Bow River in a sorry state of hunger and fatigue. Close to the Mounted Police barracks at the angle made by the two rivers, cattle were counted officially and herded across the Bow at a point now marked by the 14th Street Bridge. With no more ceremony than would mark the arrival of a bull train from Fort Macleod, Major Walker and his helpers took charge of the herd and directed it west to Big Hill where the village of Cochrane emerged later.

But misfortune was following like a Piegan stalking a stag. A few days after the herd arrived, an early storm hit the foothills and haggard cattle, still without the Cochrane brand, drifted aimlessly. Having lost much of their will to rustle, many perished in the coulees.

With spring and the odor of rotting carcasses there was a round-up and the instructions passed to the cowboys to brand every unmarked beast gathered in the sweep of the Bow Valley. Neighboring settlers, friendly up to this point, became alarmed and, in self-defence, took immediate steps to collect as many unbranded cattle as possible and burn their own marks on the hides. There was reason to believe that the Cochrane Company lost more cattle than it gained in the scramble.

THAT WAS THE FIRST COCHRANE DRIVE; the second, a year later, was equally momentous. Major Walker wanted to replenish the depleted herd and having obtained authorization to buy, rode to Montana early in 1882. Ranchers Poindexter and Orr of Dillon had cattle to sell and he went at once to inspect them. A deal was being concluded when word came of an important message awaiting Walker at Fort Benton. Suspending negotiations, he travelled back to Benton and there learned that Dr. Duncan McEachern, a company director, was recommending a complete change of plans. McEachern, never an easy person with whom to work as people about the Walrond Ranch discovered later, wanted to leave the purchase of cattle entirely to the I. G. Baker Company. Misunderstanding between Walker and McEachern had been growing for some time and this interference steeled Walker's determination to resign.

Hiding his anger, Walker returned and bought the Poindexter and Orr cattle but found the price to have increased by $25,000 because of the delay. This time, however, the vendors were to make delivery and four thousand cattle were soon on their way, making a satisfactory twelve miles a day. Poindexter, personally in charge, knew how to push the herd forward at a steady walking pace for not more than three or four hours a day, allowing the animals to graze and move at their own speed in the proper direction for most of the remaining time.

After a month and a half on the trail, the four thousand cattle in two herds were nearing Fish Creek. Indian summer had lavished its charms upon the foothills but, without warning, rough weather grabbed the scene. Wind shifted and snow came in from the northwest. Fortunately, shelter such as the trees along Fish Creek could afford was near and the cattle were urged forward to it. By the time they reached the creek, the country was in the grip of a stinging October storm.

Wind and snow continued for two days to block all trails. The herd was hemmed in. Poindexter, thinking it better to keep the cattle at the creek and let them rustle there for a time rather than drive to a snow-blanketed range around Big Hill, sent the suggestion to the Cochrane manager. Walker, probably a better policeman than cattleman, repeated the terms of an agreement to deliver the cattle without needless delays. That could mean only one thing: to continue the drive.

The experienced Montana cattleman borrowed some docile native steers from Settler John Glenn and used them to break a path through the drifts. The big herd was then collected and driven forward to Fort Calgary and Big Hill where snow was more than a foot deep on the range. The outlook for the cattle was bleak indeed and Poindexter knew it. When departing—his contractual obligations discharged—he made it very clear that he was no longer responsible for dead cattle.

Major Walker was betting on a chinook to clear the ranges, normally a good bet at that season. The chinook did come but only a brief one, crusting the snow and leaving things worse than ever. Cattle wandered along the river, eating the more tender ends of tree branches. Some appeared beside Fort Calgary and tried to break into the enclosure where hay was stacked for police horses.

Nor did things become any better as the winter advanced. Cattle died in distressing numbers. Frank White was appointed to succeed Major Walker and it was his depressing task to count the losses in the spring. Rotting beef was everywhere and the cumulative company loss at the end of the second winter was said to be a million dollars. Fewer than half the cattle purchased in Montana in the two preceding summers were still alive.

>−•◦•−<

HAVING EXPERIENCED TWO BAD WINTERS on the Bow River, company directors ruled to take the cattle to a more southerly lease between the Oldman and Waterton rivers, leaving the Bow range for sheep and horses. Hence, the Cochrane cattle were moving again and, as persistent ill luck would have it, weather conditions in the winter of 1883–'84 seemed to reverse themselves with heavy snow on the southern range and good grazing in the vicinity of Big Hill. Only by the exercise of ingenuity on the part of Frank Strong who brought the first Cochrane herd to the Bow River were heavy losses avoided in that third winter.

Any cattle company with less tenacious president and directors, or less capital, would have quit. As it was, the Cochrane outfit survived its early reverses—like a boy overcomes measles and chicken pox—and operated with success and profit until after Senator Cochrane's death in 1903 when half a million acres comprising the southern place were sold to the Mormon Church at $6.25 per acre. Ten thousand good cattle carrying the "big C" brand sold later to E. H. Maunsell and John Cowdry of Fort Macleod—a $240,000 deal.

It marked the end of a great ranching enterprise which began on one of the primitive cattle trails from the South. And, somehow, it seemed to mark the end of an era in Canadian ranching.

Cattle and Cowboys
for the "Bar U"

>━◆>━◦━<◆━<

WHILE THREE THOUSAND COCHRANE CATTLE were being driven toward the Bow River in 1881, swashbuckling Fred Stimson with the imagination of a novelist and the vocabulary of a bull skinner, was scanning the foothills and dreaming of a grassland empire. One year later, cattle for his newly formed North West Cattle Company—familiarly known in after years as the "Bar U"—were trailing out of South East Idaho, heading for the Highwood. In charge was the matchless trail-master, Tom Lynch.

Colorful Fred Stimson was one reason for unique public interest in the "Bar U" Ranch. Though a good man in a saddle, his ever-ready public pronouncements brought him at least equal fame. For the benefit of high-ranking Anglican churchmen, he announced firmly that there was something wrong with western missions; in fathering mixed blood children and improving the native stock, he explained, the Mounted Police had much more to show than the missionaries. And in an action arising from horses killed on the right-of-way, he testified that, "Any horse which can't outrun a CPR train is no good anyway and deserves to be killed."

He was living in Montreal when his brother-in-law, Superintendent William Winder, one of the "originals" in the

Mounted Police and now retired, returned to the East with glowing tales about limitless range awaiting courageous cattle-men. Stimson's curiosity was aroused. Almost at once he went to make an inspection, loved what he saw and, although still without cattle, applied for the "Bar U" brand and saw it regis-tered in his name on October 20, 1881, just when the first Cochrane cattle were nearing Big Hill.

Back at Montreal, bubbling over with enthusiasm, he talked with the Allans—Sirs Hugh and Andrew of Atlantic shipping fame—and succeeded in winning their interest in a ranching investment. Those wealthy brothers who grew up in an atmosphere of ships and shipping beside Scotland's River Clyde, had broad business connections. Sir Hugh's alleged part in the Pacific Scandal which led to the resignation of Sir John A. Macdonald's government in 1873—a case of one seeking a railroad charter making large contributions to political cam-paign funds—was now largely forgotten and Sir John was back in office.

ANYWAY, THE ALLANS—knowing no more about ranching than a bachelor is supposed to know about women's cloth-ing—were ready for any good speculative gamble and the North West Company was formed, with Fred Stimson as manager. Early in 1882, Stimson was on his way westward to buy cattle and put the plan into operation, travelling by Chicago and Fort Benton because the Canadian Pacific rails didn't go much beyond Brandon.

On a brief stop at Chicago, he bought twenty-one Shorthorn bulls and hired the first young fellow he met to care for and accompany them to the West. The slim-waisted, 19-year-old was Herb Miller from a nearby Illinois farm. What neither party to the hiring could know was that in accepting the job, Miller was starting a 52-year association with the "Bar U."

He was to take the bulls by rail to Bismarck, North Dakota, and from there by riverboat to Fort Benton where he'd leave them to be driven north to the Highwood River with a con-signment of Cochrane bulls coming shortly. Having arranged for the bulls' care at Benton, he was to proceed to the location of the company lease by any means available, and there help with construction of log buildings.

Carrying out instructions, Miller saw his bovine charges delivered at Benton by the riverboat *Black Hills*, and became a passenger on a north-bound "train" of freight wagons hauled by sixteen oxen. Travel by bull train was no faster than walking but it was safer, especially for a young fellow who was not familiar with Montana's mixed society.

In the meantime, Stimson had been at his lease on the Highwood, fixed upon a site for the headquarters, and hired Jim Meinsinger to start erecting some log shelters. At the same time, he engaged Tom Lynch to meet him at Helena, Montana, from which place they would ride together into Idaho to buy cattle. Upon Lynch would then fall the responsibility of bring-ing the herd to the Highwood.

The two men met as planned and, stirrup to stirrup, went over the mountainous country into Idaho. It was all new to Stimson but familiar to Lynch who had helped to drive Oregon cattle to mining centres in Western Montana ten years before. It was Stimson's hunch that he could buy cattle for less money in Idaho than in more accessible Montana. And sure enough, he did; in the Lost River section in the South East, he bought three thousand head showing varying degrees of longhorn character at an average price of nineteen dollars per head—also seventy-five horses for use on the thousand-mile drive that lay ahead.

At this point, Lynch took charge. His first need was a crew of reliable men for the trail. At least twenty-five riders would be needed for daytime operations, also a couple of night herders, a horse wrangler and a good cook—one with whom cowboys could live without warfare, one who would accept without thought of murder an occasional mishap like a bucking horse upsetting the ever-present stew. He hired Ab Cotterell to be foreman. That was a good beginning. Next he tried to hire Bill Moodie who had punched cows up the trail from Texas. But Moodie was indiffer-

ent about riding to Canada; at that moment he was more interested in taking trail back to Texas but he offered Lynch a proposition: "I'll go with you if you hire my friend too."

Moodie's friend was John Ware, a broad-shouldered Negro
raised in slavery. Colored boys had never distinguished themselves as horsemen or cattlemen and Lynch knew it. He was
cool to the idea but in order to get Moodie, he said: "All right,
I'll take your friend too. But can he ride a horse?"

⊳━┥◆⟩━○━⟨◆┝━⊲

JUST AFTER THE MIDDLE OF MAY, all was ready and the drive
started. At first the cattle were difficult to manage; constant
chasing and herding made men and horses extremely tired at
night. But each day brought improvement as cattle seemed to
learn what they had to do. Tom Lynch was sometimes at the
head of the long column of cattle, sometimes at the rear. John
Ware with a dilapidated saddle and half-crippled horse occupied a dusty position at the rear and Fred Stimson, after a few
days, was riding on to hasten back to the Territories.

Lynch knew exactly where to find good grazing and water
when needed. The route was close to an old trail from Oregon, then
northward on the Madison-Gallatin Trail, through rough country
and over the Continental Divide at Monida Pass. At Virginia City,
still noted for lawlessness and the ease with which the Montana
guns would go off, the men did not stop. Lynch promised time for
a cowboy celebration when they came to Helena.

Between Virginia City and Helena, John Ware made his
now-famous bid for a "betta saddle an' a li'l wuss hoss."
Whatever Moodie knew about John's riding ability, he was saying nothing and cowboys, eager for some fun, resolved to give
the big Negro a really "wuss hoss." After supper, as the sun was
sinking amid mountains, the acknowledged outlaw of the
remuda was saddled and John invited to have a ride. All hands
were there to watch the big fellow get tossed. And John, with a
sense of the dramatic, drew himself up awkwardly and said,
smilingly: "What'll ah do ef he bucks?"

No sooner was he in the saddle than the wicked horse seemed to explode skyward, kick, snort, twist in mid-air. Never had the brute been rougher. Every trick known to bucking horses was tried but John Ware stuck to the seat. Men stood in almost shocked astonishment. Never had they seen such tenacity; never had they seen a rider beat such a horse without even losing his smile. After a while the horse gave up, subdued, docile.

As John dismounted, cowboys surged around him and slapped his back as they tried to express their praise. In his modesty, John spoke only about the horse, thought it would be a good one if the same man had it every day. Tom Lynch was quick to reply: "John, he's your horse if you want him; a man who rides like that can have any horse he wants."

In after years, Lynch could boast not only of bringing the first "Bar U" cattle to Canada, but also of bringing John Ware, considered the greatest rider of his time.

>-+◆>-○-<◆+-<

AT HELENA, ONE RIDER QUIT and Ware was promoted to a more forward position, one commanding more responsibility and more respect. At this point, too, the cattle were divided into three groups of a thousand in each. They'd travel two days apart and travel better. But for each group, the day's routine was the same—grazing leisurely for two hours in the morning, then a steady drive until noon, followed by two or three hours of grazing and another two or three hours of travel before stopping for the night. They'd average twelve or thirteen miles a day that way and suffer no loss of condition.

John Ware figured in another bit of Montana drama at the Marias River where rustlers were numerous. Lynch knew he had lost some cattle, cut out in the night and driven away. John volunteered to follow the tracks. Away to the West he came upon two men heating branding irons in a coulee. Alongside was a crude corral holding cattle with a familiar appearance. Nervously, the men stood erect and drew their guns. Their faces betrayed sin but if they were like other rustlers of that time, they'd shoot rather than accept inquisition. John was in danger, but using his head. He asked where a thirsty man could get a drink of water, and before there was time for an answer, his horse bounded forward at the touch of spurs, upsetting the two men and knocking revolvers from their hands. Leaping like a cat, John was on the ground, gathering the guns and covering the desperados. It took some maneuvering but what Lynch and his men saw later was John returning, driving the stolen cattle and leading the two rustlers at the end of his lariat.

Early in September, the herds crossed the boundary and continued past Fort Whoop-Up and on to Fort Macleod where Fred Stimson was present to meet them. There the three trail herds were thrown together for the balance of the trip through an area without cultivation, without barbed wire fences and without human habitation.

Finally, on September 25, 1882, four months after leaving Lost River, Tom Lynch and his crew and cattle arrived at journey's end on the north side of the Highwood, less than a mile from where Lynch and Emerson made their first headquarters. Fred Stimson who had a herd of bulls before he had cows, and a brand before any cattle, now had cows and bulls and branding irons. Moreover, his company was now one of the two biggest cattle outfits east of the Rockies.

Tom Lynch's job was completed; most of his riders were paid off and some started the long ride back to Idaho. As for John Ware, at a hint from Lynch, Stimson offered him a permanent job and John accepted on one condition, that "yo keeps ma friend Bill Moodie too." Stimson did hire Moodie too.

>-+◆-O-◆+-<

AT FIRST THE CATTLE CARRIED the "Double Circle" brand but before long, about the time the headquarters were moved more deeply into the hills, the "Bar U" brand was adopted. In time it became the most widely known brand in all Canada, partly because the herd grew to as many as 30,000 cattle, partly because of the colorful men like Stimson, George Lane, Pat

Burns and others who were associated with it. The "Bar U" had its own individuality as news items of the early years would confirm: "Brown of Stimson's ranch," for example, meeting a grown bear in the hills and, having no gun, herded it back to the buildings the way he would a contrary bull, and there getting his gun and shooting it. Or about the "Bar U" hand, Dogie Wilder, who was attacked by a skunk while sleeping in the yard one warm night and had his nose bitten off. As Bob Edwards reported it, "He picked up the piece, stuck it on again and secured it firmly with a handkerchief bound round his head. The handkerchief was removed for the first time last Friday in the presence of an anxious group of cowpunchers. It was found that the piece had slipped and grown on his face an inch to the left of the proper position. This awkward bit of surgery has left him with one nostril in its right place and the other growing out of his cheek."

About the "Bar U" and its men there was distinct individuality.

Oxley—One of the
Great Names

>—!—‹›—‹•›—‹›—!—‹

THE OXLEY DRIVE FROM BILLINGS, MONTANA, to the ranch on
Willow Creek—five hundred miles by trail—was the ranch-
country event of 1883, just as the North West Cattle Company
drive to the Highwood made the liveliest trail history the year
before and the Cochrane drive to the Bow, two years before.

Sad to say, the exact location of the Oxley Ranch headquarters has been lost but its approximate position should not be in
dispute. It was on Willow Creek, twenty-eight stage coach
miles from Fort Macleod, thus fixing it on the easterly bulge of
the stream, northwest of the present Claresholm and almost
due west of Pulteney station.

For several years the Oxley was something of a ranchland
storm-centre, certainly a disappointment to the first manager, John
R. Craig. There was a sheriff's seizure on a grand scale when creditors became exasperated; a later manager committed suicide and
there was almost a range war when Angus Sparrow tried to collect
cattle he claimed he bought prior to a change of management.
Many times Craig must have regretted his decision to accept the
backing of cricket-playing English aristocrats instead of the
Eastern Canadians with whom he had the chance to be associated.

After trying for three years to interpret the ways of the
Canadian West for the benefit of monocled company directors,

Craig resigned and turned to a most questionable pastime: he wrote a book, called it *Ranching With Lords And Commons*.

More scholarly than most who were attracted by the cattle ranges, Craig had been secretary of the Agricultural and Arts Association of Ontario until he retired to organize a cattle company with capital he was assured of getting in Montreal; Dominion Live Stock Company, he'd call it and capitalization would be half a million dollars.

He should have held to the original plan. But when in England early in 1882, he was persuaded by A. Stavely Hill, MP for Wolverhampton, to reorganize the proposed cattle venture with English money. Everybody knew about the great and successful ranching venture in Texas and every enterprising young man found it difficult to resist the lures of raising cattle on what was almost free grass. Large amounts of British capital were being invested in Texas but good imperialists like Stavely Hill and his friends would prefer to keep their money in the Colonies. The Northwest Territories sounded inviting.

Craig yielded to the proposal to reorganize and on March 25, 1882, the Oxley Ranch Limited was formed with Hill and bushy-whiskered Lord Lathom among the directors and Craig as manager. The ranch name was taken from that of Stavely Hill's residence, Oxley Manor.

>—⬦—○—⬦—<

BACK IN CANADA, Craig obtained two leases of 100,000 acres each—one near the mouth of the Little Bow and the other extending into the Porcupine Hills—then proceeded west via Helena, Montana. At that place he hired some men and started north over the four hundred miles of trail, receiving an initiation in sleeping on soogans spread on the ground and doing all "housekeeping" chores beside a wagon.

Making camp beside Willow Creek, he set the men to building some shelters and putting up hay. Craig wasn't a pessimist but he believed it wise to have some winter feed in stacks, even in the chinook belt. Apart from one hundred and sixteen horses driven from British Columbia by a man named Rush and bought at seventy dollars a head, Craig was still without livestock when he heard at the first of September that Stavely Hill was coming to see his "raunch." Perhaps it appeared like the prospective visit from a wealthy mother-in-law but Craig drove to meet the man and escort him to Willow Creek where log buildings were arising.

On the day of arrival at the ranch, September 25th—also the very day on which the first "Bar U" cattle arrived at their new range on the Highwood—Hill saw the second herd of Cochrane cattle moving northward on the trail and was very much impressed, as a paragraph in his book, From Home to Home, makes clear: "... we caught sight of a large herd of cattle and on coming down to meet the wagons that were with them, we heard we were close to Willow Creek. The herd which we had come across was one of forty-five hundred, in two bands nearly equally divided; they had been bought down in the South from Mr. Senator Cochrane and were being driven up to his range near Calgary. This was my first view of a large band of cattle and a very beautiful sight it was."

After a drive back into the Porcupines to shoot and see the company range—and near disaster in the same storm which trapped the Cochrane cattle at Fish Creek—Stavely Hill announced his intention of accompanying Craig to Montana for the purpose of buying cattle. The member of Parliament for Wolverhampton was ready for the five hundred-mile trip to Billings by team and buckboard, and the ranch manager had no choice but to express his "delight."

>──I─◆>─◆─O─◆<─I──<

THE FIRST STOP WAS AT FORT MACLEOD and while Hill was not impressed by "the town represented by a wide, muddy lane, with a row of dirty, half-finished wooden shanties flanking each side," he was very much impressed by "Kamoose" Taylor at whose "Hotel Macleod" he spent the night. About the unconventional host, he wrote, "Mr. Henry

Taylor had originally begun life as a missionary but having given up that profession, came in from Montana with the whisky traders in 1872 and distinguished himself a good deal in that line. ... While engaged in business as a whisky trader, he had stolen a woman from one of the Bloods, though according to his own account, he had not stolen her but had traded her for a gallon of whisky; but however that may be, he was not allowed to remain in peaceful possession of the lady as the Blood from whom he had stolen her was on his trail, intending to kill him and the woman; and as Kamoose prudently observed, there was no use in having anybody killed about it; he thought that the best thing he could do was to pass her on and so he traded her to somebody else—perhaps one of the Bloods—for half a gallon of whisky. The Bloods, however, nicknamed him Kamoose, signifying in their language, "robber."

Three weeks later, Hill and Craig came to the ranch of Higgins and McCain on Montana's Dupuyer Creek and fancied the cattle there offered for sale. Craig, considered an especially good judge of livestock, said these were superior to any which had preceded them onto the Canadian range. He advised buying them and in order to have a place for them until spring, buying the ranch also. This they did—bought ranch, about twenty-five hundred cattle and one hundred and sixty horses—and Hill wrote a cheque for $115,000.

From Billings, Hill took train to the East and started his journey back to England, satisfied that his ranching investment would shortly pay big dividends. Craig turned his democrat horses to the North and retraced the long trail back to Oxley Ranch. But there wasn't much to hold him there and in December he drove again to Montana—just like going to town for the mail. On the first of January, 1883, he was back at Dupuyer Creek and buying nine hundred and seventy-nine more cattle from one man, three hundred and five from another, bringing the Oxley herd total to thirty-five hundred head.

He was anxious to be on the trail for the North as early in the spring season as possible but, first, he'd have to find his cat-

tle running on the limitless Prairies. Having a big stake in the
Montana round-up, he and five men hired for the drive joined
in the big spring operation, Montana-style—quite an experience for a man who had been secretary of an Agricultural and
Arts Association.

But Craig gave a good account of himself, riding with the
seasoned cattlemen, and as soon as round-up was over, he was
ready for the drive to Willow Creek. Momentarily, his only
embarrassment was that money with which to pay for the last
cattle bought had not arrived from England and he was obliged
to borrow from I. G. Baker Company at the atrocious interest
rate of one percent per month.

>-+<>-·-O-·-<+-+-<

IN JUNE, CRAIG'S HERD WERE TOGETHER at Muddy River—
thirty-four hundred head altogether and still about two hundred and fifty miles from Oxley Ranch. But with him were
men who had accompanied Poindexter in the previous year
and could offer experience. Twelve miles a day was their
usual rate of travel, except when there was a river to cross or
an argument with Indians. The biggest delay occasioned by
Natives was at the South Piegan Reserve where a ten cents
per head toll was demanded for crossing. Craig paid it—
three hundred and forty-dollars—reasoning that, unreason-
able as it seemed, it was still better than having to detour
around the reservation.

On July 25th Craig and his crew were at the St. Mary's
River, under the gaze of three Mounted Policemen sta-
tioned there to watch for whisky runners and check
incoming cattle. While officers made the official count,
Craig's riders relaxed and their thoughts turned to entertainment. Good Methodist Craig would forbid gambling
but there was no rule against a bit of horse racing. Every
cowboy with a string of seven or eight horses had one
with enough speed to give him a show in a quarter-mile
roadside contest.

A race developed between Craig's men and those of another cowboy outfit camping nearby. One of Craig's helpers with a pistol volunteered to be the starter—evidently with an ulterior motive, that of killing "two birds with one stone." When he fired, he not only started the race but shot a rival cowboy for whom he had no fondness. Mounties stepped forward to arrest the culprit, but he leaped into his saddle and galloped toward the International Border on a horse which proved too fast for the police. Once on the Montana side, he called across inviting the Mounties to take his fond regards back to Craig and ask him to forward his mail to Fort Benton.

With no less than usual difficulty, the thirty-four hundred cattle were forced across the St. Mary River. Craig recognized the picturesque qualities of the scene—thirty-four hundred horned heads in the water, then out on the other side, calves bawling, cows fretting and all dripping.

And two days after making the crossing, the cowboy fugitive responsible for the unauthorized shooting returned to continue the drive, just as though nothing unusual had happened. The herd crossed Lee's Creek—still four years before the first Mormon settlers arrived—crossed the Blood Reserve, passed Stand-off and swam the Belly, Waterton and Oldman rivers, practically following Alberta's Number Two Highway of a later date, and arrived at the Oxley about August 1st. Calves born along the way—some transported by wagon—were now branded with the OX irons, and everything turned out to get fat on the belly-deep grass.

>─►◆─○─◄◆─◄

CRAIG HAD REASON TO BE PLEASED with progress but his troubles were far from being over. Stavely Hill and Lord Lathom came on one of the first passenger trains from Winnipeg to Calgary, on August 30th. They authorized the purchase of four thousand more cattle but nothing brought more than temporary relief in meeting current payments. Craig was being blamed for failure to settle accounts and in May, 1885, the sheriff seized three thousand Oxley cattle and three hundred horses and advertised their sale to meet certain debts. It was humiliating but at the last minute money came from England and the sale was stopped.

Craig went to England to face his uncomprehending colleague, but it didn't achieve much. He was accused of buying inferior stock. Soon after returning to the ranch, he resigned. The Oxley was reorganized and rechristened New Oxley, and continued its unsteady course under the management of Australian-born Stanley Pinhorn. But in spite of tribulations, Oxley was one of the great names in Canadian ranching and the Oxley drive of 1883 was one to be remembered for its success.

Horse Trouble on the Trail

ANY BOREDOM WHICH MAY HAVE EXISTED in the 1884 community beside Fort Calgary vanished like a morning mist the day Michael Oxarart drove in with a band of two hundred Oregon and Montana horses. Trail herds and elongated bull trains were fairly common thereabout, but the man Oxarart was uncommon at any time or place and during the weeks following his arrival neither the peaceful citizens nor the Mounted Police could make up their minds if the lean and swarthy Frenchman was a gentleman or a horsethief.

In any case, the horse drive which began in Oregon and ended at Brandon was a frontier epic. And at one point in the turbulent events there was well-founded fear that Oxarart's trouble with Canadian authorities might explode into international dispute.

Oxarart, from the Pyrenees of Southern France, migrated to Texas and adopted the cowboy life as a flea adopts a dog. Like many other adventuresome sons of the stock saddle, he rode north into Montana and, in 1883, into the Northwest Territories. In his mind as he travelled was the hope of finding a really choice ranch location for himself, and what he saw on the southern slope of Cypress Hills led him to erect a log cabin intended to give him a squatter's claim to the nearby grass. He would return, he vowed—return to raise horses.

The growing demand for work stock in the homestead country where most settlers were short of power, suggested opportunity and Oxarart resolved to come with a band of sale horses. After wintering in Oregon, the irrepressible Frenchman and his helper, Charlie Thebo, were starting from near the interior of that State with one hundred bronchos. How the animals were acquired is not known and speculation will achieve nothing.

>─┤◆>─○─<◆┤─<

THE FACT WAS THAT THE TWO HORSEMEN were on the trail, their destination unknown. About the end of June, with four hundred miles of trail behind them, they rode into the Town of Macleod, dutifully presented themselves before the officer of the Canadian Customs and announced readiness to pay the necessary import tax on one hundred horses. The officer made an official count, accepted Oxarart's valuation of $35 per head, and collected the assessment. There was no argument, no hesitation.

Oxarart was a friendly fellow and within a few days knew all the people in the town. Before departing, he and D. W. Davis of the I. G. Baker Company rode to inspect the imported bronchos grazing on the river flats and agreed they would sell readily to settlers flocking to the country, especially in that part between Regina and Brandon.

"Any chance you'd be interested in buying another hundred head and taking them along too?" Davis enquired. "You could sell two hundred about as easily as a hundred out there in Assiniboia."

Oxarart was interested and before leaving he made a deal for the additional stock which the I. G. Baker Company had brought from the South and on which, presumably, the customs duty was paid in full.

Oxarart and Thebo, with no worries, gathered the enlarged band together and turned it on the Calgary Trail. They rode close to the Oxley Ranch headquarters where a house was under construction, passed a freight wagon drawn by sixteen oxen, forded the Highwood River and lesser streams, and came into Calgary with the idea of resting there for a couple of days—perhaps even selling a few horses.

But before the horseman had time to price a horse or buy a drink, Customs Officer Bannerman, who was also the local postmaster, noticed the horse band had more animals than the number on which Oxarart was known to have paid duty.

"Crooked work," concluded the officer, not knowing anything about the purchase made from the I. G. Baker Company. "Smuggling, to be sure!" Acting upon impulse, Bannerman ordered seizure of the whole herd.

The Frenchman shouted protests as only a Frenchman can, but the officer, welcoming a chance to exercise his authority, refused to listen. He did not release the stock until Customs Officer Cotton and D. W. Davis drove from Fort Macleod to identify the horses and vouch for Oxarart's legitimate purchase of half the band on the Canadian side. It took time but in the end the local officer was obliged to admit error in judgment. The horses were released, reluctantly.

⪼ ⊶ ◦ ⊷ ⪻

THE NEXT MISTAKE WAS OXARART'S, in failing to drive the released horses out of Calgary in a hurry. He should have realized how Customs Officers resent any suggestion of fallibility. Almost at once, Bannerman sensed another reason for his persistent suspicion: that Oxarart's imported horses at $35 per head were under-valued for purposes of the duty. Again he instructed the Mounted Police to seize them and hold them until the horseman made an acceptable adjustment.

The proceedings were doing nothing to improve the Frenchman's temper. He wished he had never seen Calgary. Nor would he accept the charge that he had misrepresented the value in making declaration. He was mad and after more days of annoying delay, Officer Bannerman was again obliged to acknowledge a mistaken hunch and instruct the sheriff to release the controversial bronchos.

But at this point, the Customs Officer found himself in a position of double embarrassment; forty-five of the horses were missing, having disappeared while being held under order. "Stolen and run across the line," was the common conclusion. At once Oxarart charged laxity and waxed loud in his denunciation of the Canadian authorities. Bannerman, at the same time, was in the humiliating position of an officer on the defensive and was saying nothing.

Everybody on Stephen Avenue heard Oxarart proclaim that the government men, in seizing his horses without proper cause, had to be fully responsible for any losses. If the horses were stolen while held by the deputy sheriff, the government would have to pay for them—"pay in full," shouted the angry man. If there was hesitation, he would carry his case to the government of the United States.

It was now late in August and Oxarart was anxious to get on his way toward Brandon. But before leaving Calgary, he had to deliver sixty of the horses to nearby Mount Royal Ranch, sale of this number having been made while the horse herd was under seizure. It seemed like a perfectly legitimate transaction.

Having sold sixty head and lost forty-five to the sheriff, Oxarart was down to about ninety or ninety-five, but he started eastward on the trail to Medicine Hat, Moose Jaw and Brandon, happy to be leaving Calgary behind. He hoped he'd never see the place again. Most foothills people who had been watching with interest, were generally sympathetic toward the man and were sorry to see him leave. But they hadn't heard the last of the confusing case, not by any means.

Refreshed after a long delay, Oxarart and Thebo and their horses made good time on the trail to Assiniboia. They halted briefly at Maple Creek, to which place the Frenchman intended to return sooner or later to conduct full scale ranching operations. Continuing, the men sold a few horses along the way but were keeping the main part of the stock for Brandon where the demand was said to be brisk.

ON AN EARLY SEPTEMBER DATE, the *Moose Jaw News* reported, "Mr. Oxarart is in town with over eighty head of horses which he has brought in from Oregon by way of Calgary." Fourteen or fifteen more horses were sold to Moose Jaw buyers and again the outfit was on the way, making fast time. About a week later, men and horses were at journey's end and the *Brandon Sun* (Sept. 18, 1884) reported, "Mr. Oxarart arrived on Saturday from Oregon, by way of Calgary with between seventy and eighty horses. They are a fine looking lot … he finds sales rapid."

It was the end of a fifteen hundred-mile trail journey for Michael Oxarart and Charlie Thebo but it wasn't the end of this trouble-packed episode and before the *Brandon Sun* reached its readers, Oxarart and Thebo were under arrest. Bannerman and the Mounted Police boys back at Calgary had not been idle. They seemed to share a premonition that Oxarart was guilty—of something. When the zealous Customs Officer drove into the country to take a second look at the sixty horses Oxarart sold to Mount Royal Ranch, he made a discovery: instead of sixty horses on the ranch with the Oxarart brand—"fleur-de-lis"—there were one hundred and five. He was good at arithmetic; sixty horses sold plus forty-five horses stolen when the band was in custody made a total of one hundred and five. Bannerman and the police jumped at the conclusion that Oxarart himself had stolen the horses—stolen his own property from inside the sheriff's sealed fence. Again official orders were issued and all of the one hundred and five horses were seized. Moreover, a charge was laid and the police arrested both Oxarart and Thebo just a matter of hours after their arrival at Brandon.

As reported in the *Nor'-Wester* published in Calgary, "Mr. Oxarart and his foreman, Thebo, were arrested at Brandon at the instance of Sub-Collector of Customs Bannerman, on a charge of attempting to defraud the Revenue by making away with forty-five horses which were supposed to have been stolen."

A few days later, Oxarart and Thebo appeared before Mounted Police Inspector Dowling in Calgary, were charged with larceny, and committed for trial. But the evidence submitted was fragmentary and ultimately both men were acquitted.

As for the one hundred and five horses, sixty of them were counted back at random to the Mount Royal Ranch and forty-five were retained by the authorities while Oxarart repeated that he was calling for the full weight of United States might to see that compensation was paid for the confiscated animals.

For the people of Calgary it was the best entertainment of the year and they were sorry to think the chapter might be about to end. The extraordinary horseman went back to Brandon to sell his horses and was there for several months The *Brandon Sun* of January 8, 1885, noted that, "On New Year's night a horse worth $150 was raffled at the Royal Hotel. Mr. Oxarart was the winner." Some people with suspicious minds wondered if the same Mr. Oxarart had also organized the raffle.

>-·◄►·-·O-·◄►·-·◄

HAVING SOLD THE LAST OF HIS BRONCHOS, Oxarart went back to Montana, got more horses and came back in the spring, this time to stock his new ranch in the Cypress Hills. In embarking upon ranching, the cavalier Frenchman meant business. Obviously, Canadian authorities had given him trouble but he was a forgiving soul and grew to love his adopted grass country. His stock increased until he was the biggest producer of horses between Winnipeg and Medicine Hat. For the most part he used Morgan sires but he also bred Thoroughbreds and for a number of years sent some of the fastest horses to the race meets in the Territories and Manitoba.

In 1896, health failing, Michael Oxarart left to visit his native France but he died on the way. D. J. "Joe" Wylie bought the ranch in the Hills.

And Charlie Thebo? He went back to the Northern States but in 1898 the name appeared as one taking Washington State cattle over the Dalton Trail to far-away Dawson City. Had his old trail-mate been alive, no doubt he'd have been driving horses over the same hazardous route and entertaining or worrying

everybody with whom he made contact. And exercising his practised skill in staying just a short distance ahead of the law, he'd
be the object of occasional glances from the Mounted Police.

Benton Bronks for Regina

❧ ⟶ ✦ ⟶ ⊙ ⟵ ✦ ⟵ ❧

REGINA'S TALL AND RAMROD-STRAIGHT ROBERT SINTON—nearly
a hundred years old when he died—could tell of walking most
of the way from Rapid City to Pile of Bones in 1882, about
freighting to the scene of the Duck Lake war in 1885, and dick-
ering to sell land for the site of Saskatchewan's Legislative
Building; and with special zest he related the adventures on a
four hundred and fifty mile trail over which he drove Montana
horses for sale at Regina in 1886.

"Driving horses in those days was more dangerous than
driving cattle," he explained, "especially in Montana where men
of the outlaw breed would sometimes shoot a horseman and
steal his stock." The point was that horses, more than cattle,
could be whisked away from the scene of a crime and hidden in
some remote coulee. They were more maneuverable, more
fluid, more like currency with trading value anywhere.

A man with a band of horses could expect to make good
time on the trail and in that respect he was the envy of cattlemen. But day and night he had added worries. If cattle strayed
at night, at least they weren't likely to be far away in the morning; horses, on the other hand, might be far removed in any
direction by sunrise.

And when Sinton was driving across the Montana and
Saskatchewan plains, there was neither fence nor farm-yard

corral from which he might get aid in holding a wild band at night. The hope, as the old stockman explained, was to drive for at least twenty or twenty-five miles during the day so that horses would be tired at night. Then, after an hour or so of late evening grazing, even the wild ones were ready to settle and remain quietly for the hours of darkness.

"Just the same," Robert Sinton added, "we always had one man on guard through the nights. Nobody like night-herding; the hours were long and lonely and coyote howls sent shivers down the bravest man's spine. But we were young and if we had been afraid of adventure, we wouldn't have been in the West at that time."

OF PIONEER EXPERIENCES—MANY AND VARIED—those related to horses and cattle were closest to Robert Sinton's heart and nobody deserved more fully to be called the father of the live-stock industry in Saskatchewan. He was the first president of the Saskatchewan Stock Breeders' Association and almost half a century later he was honorary president of the Saskatchewan Livestock Board. In the area now described as southern Saskatchewan, he was the first to breed purebred Hereford cat-tle and the records show him as one of the first contributors of Herefords to the Calgary Bull Sale. Many times he crossed the Atlantic to buy Clydesdales and in 1920 when the government of Saskatchewan was prepared to invest in one or more out-standing Scottish stallions, Robert Sinton, Dean Rutherford, and William Gibson were the men delegated to make the selec-tion. But before Sinton was a breeder of show animals, he was a homesteader and before the Regina settlers thought seriously about pedigrees, they wanted work stock—ordinary work horses for the slugging on Prairie homesteads, and Sinton was game to ride for them even if it meant dodging some lawless Montana gangs.

Sinton had been at Regina four years when he went for the horses and already knew much about roughing it. At the age of twenty-four he left home in the province of Quebec, came into Winnipeg by riverboat and took a homestead at Rapid City, guessing that the new transcontinental railroad would touch that place. But the rails did not go that way and in 1882—after four years on the homestead—he decided to move again to the West and gamble once more on a railroad location.

At Pile of Bones, he found excitement; men at this tent town beside the creek had learned that their place would not only be on the railroad but Hon. Edgar Dewdney had chosen it to be the site for the territorial capital.

Sinton took a job putting up hay for the Mounted Police and assured himself that Pile of Bones had a bright future, despite certain strong views to the contrary. Fifty years later, as Sinton's Regina prepared for the World's Grain Show in that city, the pioneer was carrying a clipping from the Manitoba Daily Free Press of September 1, 1882, commenting that, "Whether Regina ever becomes the capital or not, one thing is certain—it will never amount to anything more than a country village or town for the simple reason that in neither its position nor its sur- roundings is there anything to give it the slightest commercial importance. Situated in the midst of a vast plain of inferior soil with hardly a tree to be seen as far as the eye can range, and with about enough water in the miserable little creek known as Pile of Bones to wash a sheep, it would scarcely make a respectable farm, to say nothing of being fixed upon as the site for the capi- tal of a great province. The place has not a single natural advan- tage to commend it."

When trouble took the form of rebellion near Duck Lake, Sinton volunteered to haul ammunition by team and wagon to the fighting front. It was an anxious time and anyone on the trails wanted to be well armed because any clump of poplars could be hiding hostile half-breeds or sympathetic Indians. But Sinton escaped without injury and when the war ended, he con- tinued for months to do freighting for the Mounted Police.

>-+◆>-O-<+-I-<

HENCE, IN 1886, when he decided to bring horses from Montana, he was no stranger to the trails—at least, not on the Canadian side where he knew every camping place offering wood and water. Montana, its trails still unknown to him, was a different matter but rumor that broncho horses—not quite as wild as antelope—could be bought at $30 in the part between Fort Benton and Helena rang like a challenge. Settlers needed horses urgently and he needed the money he might make by selling such bronchos for $60 a head after chasing them across the plains.

With roll of blankets, pack of food, loaded rifle strapped to the saddle and a good bay mare under him, Sinton set out boldly like Samson after the Philistines. Spring filled the air as he rode southwesterly to Wood Mountain and crossed the boundary. Almost at once he had a rude introduction to Montana's rougher element. Rain was falling and wet clothes clung to his chilled skin when he decided to seek shelter for the night at an isolated cabin on the Prairies. He knocked at the shattered door, knocked again; then it opened slightly on its rawhide hinges and out came the muzzle of a gun.

"What you want?" a man whose face remained hidden enquired in a low and sullen tone.

"Pardon me," Sinton stammered as doubts about what he really did want welled up within him. "I was just wondering if you'd let me sleep inside, out of this rain."

There was a pause and the gruff voice sounded again: "You can sleep in the stable."

It wasn't a comfortable night, what with rain coming through the stable roof and speculation about the mystery man in the cabin. But early in the morning, without stopping to say "farewell" to his host, Sinton was cantering west. The gun and the gruff voice, Sinton learned later, belonged to a character known only as Dutch Henry. It was a name which became better and better known for its connection with crime, however. Dutch Henry was blamed for stealing numerous horses from settlers around Willow Bunch and running them across the line. What happened to him ultimately wasn't clear; one story had him killed in a Montana gunfight, another, that with the police on his trail, he skipped to South America.

Sinton's course took him through Havre, Fort Benton and into Sun River country where he bought one hundred and fifty horses with mixed colors showing Indian stock on one side and more than average size and quality reflecting imported breeds on the other. A helper was hired and the wild band was headed toward Fort Benton.

While still in the Sun River Valley, Sinton paused at a half-breed community and entered into conversation with a friendly big fellow, robust and obviously quite intelligent. The stranger learned with interest that Sinton was from Canada and said he too was a Canadian— "from Batoche, on the South Saskatchewan."

When it was time to part, Sinton extended his hand, asked the man his name and was a little shocked to hear him say, "Dumont—Gabriel Dumont." Here, to be sure, was Louis Riel's chief lieutenant, the real fireball in the so-called rebellion of the year before, wanted by the Canadian authorities.

>-+>-O-<+-<

AT FORT BENTON, the horsemen turned to the north and then took the trail branching to Fort Walsh in the Cypress Hills. All was going well, twenty-five miles a day, until another typical Montana situation blew up like a squall on Long Lake. It was near Fort Assiniboine, northwest of Bear's Paw Mountains. Sinton was preparing a meal on the grass between the trail and a small river, when armed men, their faces half hidden by dirt and whiskers, rode up and demanded to see the bill-of-sale covering the horses he was driving. Vigilantes they were, settlers taking the law in their own hands, and out to stop rustling and other crimes.

To the Canadian, they didn't look any better than ordinary desperados and, this being his first trip for horses, he had over-looked the importance of getting documentary proof of purchase. He had to confess that he had no bill-of-sale and the strangers interpreted this as clear evidence of theft. They meant business. The leader asked a few perfunctory questions but without waiting for the answers, one of the ruffians pointed to a cotton-wood tree at the river and mumbled that the same one had been used on other occasions.

The trial, if such it could be called, was over. A rope was uncoiled and Sinton was being escorted in the direction of the hangman tree. Any man who couldn't prove where he got a band of horses was guilty and any horse thief had to be hung. It was as simple as that. Sinton was making protests but nobody was listening and time was running out when, by a streak of much-needed luck, Jim Henderson, the very man from whom the purchase was made, came that way and recognized the horses and Sinton.

"Take your hands off this man," Henderson shouted, drawing his pistol to make the command more convincing. "Of course he bought the horses, bought them from me and paid cash. Besides, he's a Canadian. Now be done with your damned mistakes."

That settled it and none too soon. The vigilante leader apologized and hastened to inform Sinton that he too had horses for sale. But Sinton was glad to be back on the trail to the north, glad to be crossing the border and approaching the Cypress Hills. Now, he was in a familiar setting once again, and nearing home.

By the time he reached Regina the horses seemed measurably more docile. At any rate, settlers needed them urgently and bought them readily. Some kicked democrats to splinters and some ran away with seed drills, but most of them settled down to become useful farm horses.

><+>+O+<+><

REMEMBERING THAT THE CANADIAN GOVERNMENT had placed a price on the head of Gabriel Dumont, Sinton sought out Col. Irvine of the Mounted Police and told him about the surprise meeting near Sun River. The police officer listened attentively, looked seriously and said, "Just forget about him. We're glad to leave him there." Shortly after that, the former rebel went on tour in the United States and Europe with Buffalo Bill.

Robert Sinton, at that time thirty-two years of age, should have considered himself lucky to be back and in good health. Evidently the experiences of the trail didn't worry him because he went back to Montana for more horses—and went again.

Northward Toward Saskatoon

THE CART TRAIL CUT BY TEMPERANCE COLONY SETTLERS—whisky-hating Methodists—making their way from Moose Jaw to the site of Saskatoon in 1883, marked the route taken by John Mawson and other cattlemen searching for greener pastures three years later.

The Mawson drive consisting of two hundred cattle was inspired by sheer necessity, there being almost no feed in the Moose Jaw district. Drought led to near crop-failure in 1884—the Ontario man's second year in the West—and again in 1885. When the season of 1886 promised to be even more austere, Mawson, whose cattle had multiplied to over one hundred head, admitted the necessity of moving with his herd. Cattlemen had to be resourceful. But where could he go?

It was late in June when he hitched two broncho horses to the family buckboard and set out to find better cattle range. He drove southwesterly to Wood Mountain, thence northwesterly to Swift Current and back to Moose Jaw. On the two hundred-mile triangle tour he saw good tree shelter, he encountered places well provided with water, and he drove over inviting grass, but he did not find all three of these cow-country prerequisites in combination.

Taking a fresh supply of bacon and flour and a change of horses, Mawson set out again, this time driving northward in the direction of the Temperance Colony called Saskatoon. After five days of travel through unsettled country and five nights spent under the democrat, he came to what was later called Proctor's Lake, west of the present Dundurn. Here, surely, was the land of a cattleman's dreams. Here was the combination of natural conditions for which he had been searching—grass, water and shelter.

"This place was created for cattle," Mawson said to himself. "This is the place for me."

>─◂▸─O─◂▸─◂

AS HE WAS HURRYING BACK TO MOOSE JAW to get haying equipment, Mawson met the Browns from Regina and the Mutches from Lumsden, likewise searching for a grassy place to which they and their cattle might escape from the famine brought on by drought. Generously, Mawson informed the travellers about his fortunate discovery and that they would find more grass back there than they had ever seen between Regina and Lumsden. And back at Moose Jaw, he told Settlers Joseph Proctor and Hon. W. A. Holmes a'Court, both of whom had sizeable herds.

Not waiting to confirm by their own inspection of the north-country grass one hundred and twenty-five miles away, Proctor and a'Court loaded mowing machines and started over the trail several days before Mawson could get organized for the same sort of haymaking expedition. But the two eccentric Englishmen became lost enroute and Mawson was cutting hay at the destination before they arrived.

With sufficient hay in stacks, the Moose Jaw men returned to bring on their cattle. Proctor and a'Court made preparations to move permanently. Mawson, on the other hand, gathered cattle from all his Moose Jaw neighbors, agreeing to winter them along with his own and bring them back in the spring. He was offering to do everything—drive the cattle almost as far as

Saskatoon, furnish hay for the winter and drive them back in the spring—for $5 per head. Nobody could accuse the cattle-man of being greedy.

The composite herd of two hundred cattle was neither uni-form nor handsome. There were animals of all known colors and types. There were some with long horns telling of southern ancestry, some with short horns which came from Ontario, and some with no horns at all. Most of them were wild and ready to run but others showed the docility of family milk cows. "They didn't even bawl the same way," the cattleman said.

Mawson knew very well that some parts of the drive would be difficult, even dangerous, especially the first portion of the route over which all sloughs were so dry that gophers were dig-ging holes at their centres. In that season of hot weather, the absence of water for thirsty cattle and horses could present very serious problems.

From Moose Jaw the trail bore north and northwesterly toward the Elbow of the South Saskatchewan River, and then north again. The trail ruts were still comparatively fresh, the first of the Temperance Colony settlers having travelled that way as recently as three summers before and taken the very first cattle across those plains. The idea of a settlement safely removed from all the evils of alcohol had its beginning at Toronto in 1881. The C.P.R. was built as far as Brandon at that time and the Canadian government, dissatisfied with the num-ber of homesteaders going west, announced willingness to sell blocks of land to colonization societies.

"Here's our chance," the Methodist promoters said enthu-siastically, "a settlement securely isolated by distance from all the foul odors and temptations of sinful John Barleycorn."

Application was made for land and the government allotted some three hundred sections straddling the South Saskatchewan River. J. N. Lake and two other officers went at once to make inspection and on August 20, 1882, they camped on the site of the centre they intended to call Minnetonka, until a Sunday afternoon when Lake was presented with a handful of berries described as saskatoons. So impressed was the Society leader by the flavorful fruit that he proclaimed at once: "Arise Saskatoon, Queen of the North."

⋗⋅⟡⋅○⋅⟡⋅⋖

IN APRIL OF THE NEXT SPRING, 1883, Moose Jaw saw the Temperance Colony settlers leaving the new railroad cars and preparing for the one hundred and fifty-five mile trail trip to the "Promised Land." As the newcomers departed with loaded wagons, green horses and worried expressions, there were a few tragedies. Before the horses became sufficiently exhausted to perform reliably, some ran away, scattering plows, hens and bags of flour on the plains. Oxen, obstinate at the best of times, dragged loaded wagons to the middle of nearby draws and lay down to cool their bellies. Wagons broke down and, as though the ordinary vicissitudes of the trail were not enough, there was a night blizzard that lifted tents and left families exposed to the driving snow.

And the first cattle to be delivered at Saskatoon were being driven over the trail with that cavalcade of homeseekers. Teenager John Kusch, having accepted the responsibility of driving all the milk cows—fifteen or twenty of them—walked the one hundred and fifty-five miles or more during the thirty days between April 19 and May 19, 1883.

And so, the cattle with which Mawson started north were not the first to go over the trail but they constituted the first sizeable herd. Mounted on two poorly trained horses, Mawson and one helper turned the herd away from Moose Jaw Creek at midday and drove as briskly as safety would allow through the hot afternoon.

The country was dry; there was no doubt about it. There being no cultivation along the way, drifting soil was practically unknown but grass was so short and parched that it could neither afford fair grazing nor hide the abundant buffalo bones appearing everywhere with a sepulchre-like whiteness. By sundown, the cattle were obviously thirsty but there was no water in sight. Even White's Slough was dry and Mawson knew he was still many miles from relief. After a short stop for rest, the herd was pressed forward again and in the dim light of the Prairie moon, travel continued all night.

At sunrise the men breathed with relief when they recognized the upper Qu'Appelle Valley and knew they were close to the little stream which threaded its way along the floor. It was a fifty-two mile drive from Moose Jaw to this particular point where the trail intersected the stream, Mawson figured, but now, after the trials of that night, there was no longer any particular reason for hurrying.

The trail continued along the valley to the elbow of the South Saskatchewan and there was water as well as feed to meet the immediate needs.

North of the Elbow, however, were more dry places but the effect of drought was less obvious than at Moose Jaw. A few sloughs had water and one homesteader or squatter had a well from which water could be lifted by means of bucket and rope. For Mawson, the last night camp before reaching the grassy marsh west of today's Dundurn was the homestead cabin of Robert Wilson, forty-five miles south of Saskatoon and six miles west of the present Hanley. The Wilsons, including sons Russell, James and Archie who became leaders in Saskatchewan, were from Carlton County in Ontario, and had arrived to farm beside the Moose Jaw trail about the same time as the first Temperance Colony people came. Later, they too took to ranching in the country west of Dundurn.

>━┥◆〉━○━〈◆┝━<

AND WHILE MAWSON WAS DRIVING HIS HERD northward late in the summer of 1886, two other young cattlemen were making history on the same trail. Joseph and Robert Caswell who came with the first group of Temperance Colony settlers were now bringing the first purebred cattle to the Saskatoon district. The Shorthorn cows and bull had been shipped from Ontario and the Caswell boys were hoping to have their bovine blue-bloods at Saskatoon in time for the first fall fair. The cows were being herded over the trail in the customary manner but the aristocratic red sire with lazy fat on his back seemed to warrant more tender care and was being transported all the way from Moose Jaw to Saskatoon in a farm wagon hauled by two Caswell horses.

Triumphantly, those pioneer purebreds made their public appearance at the Saskatoon fair and had no trouble in winning admiration and the one dollar prize for the best herd, while John Kusch won the special award of one dollar in the class for trotting ox hitched to buckboard and "Bowman's one-eyed cayuse" won the dollar prize in the one-mile horse race. In the two-mile horse race, the first prize was the more munificent sum of two dollars—a dollar-a-mile basis, it seemed.

Mawson didn't see that first Saskatoon fair although exactly two years earlier he exhibited at Moose Jaw's fair and collected a handsome brace of four first prizes, for calf of the current year, daughter Nellie entered in the baby show, a pan of home-made bread of Mrs. Mawson's making, and ox-team race conducted on the main street. Of more immediate importance, ten days after leaving Moose Jaw, he and his cattle—all in good health—were at journey's end where water was abundant, shelter assured, and hay in stacks adequate for winter's normal needs. He was still without a shelter for himself but there were trees nearby and instead of taking in the Saskatoon fair, he was creating a cabin.

The plan was a good one but that winter of 1886–'87 proved to be the most severe in a lifetime. Fully half of the cattle on the western ranges perished. Mawson's cattle, with shelter and sufficient feed, wintered fairly well.

IN THE SPRING OF 1887, he drove the herd back over the trail to Moose Jaw, but before long he was going again to Dundurn, going to stay and raise cattle alongside W. A. H. a'Court whose herd grew to seven hundred head, and Joseph Proctor, the well-whiskered graduate of England's best schools who ran up to five hundred head. In that grass country between Dundurn and the South Saskatchewan River, John Mawson wasn't the biggest ranch operator but it was he, unquestionably, who "discovered" the area, sensed its suitability for cattle, and then piloted the first herds to it.

The Senator's Sheep

TO THE CATTLEMEN OF THE OLD RANGE, sheep were an abomination and sheep herders didn't rate much higher. By their grazing habits, the "woolies" left nothing for cattle and there could be no room for both kinds on the same grass. When sheep herders intruded, range climate became perfect for local warfare. Cowboys could understand why Abel, "a keeper of sheep," was slain by Cain.

Cattlemen hoping to safeguard their grass resources and at the same time minimize the incidence of murder, requested the government to force exclusion of sheep from the ranching area. The South Western Stock Association was their mouthpiece while the new Calgary Agricultural Society, acting mainly for the farmer settlers, held views to the contrary and urged that sheep breeding be encouraged. The Canadian government, pursuing the ancient art of compromise, acted in 1884 to bar sheep in the south while granting all the blessings of freedom north of the Highwood River.

This arrangement suited the Cochrane Ranch interests perfectly. By creating a subsidiary company they could qualify for a second lease of a hundred thousand acres and raise cattle in the south and sheep in the north. After the experience of two bad winters on the Bow River range, the Cochrane cattle had been taken to grass beside the Belly, leaving the hills west of Calgary for an experiment with some other class of livestock. Moreover, Senator Cochrane was known to be influential at Ottawa and ranchland spectators wondered how much he had to do with the plan that left his former cattle range in a position to invite sheep. Even before the new regulations were passed, preparations were being made to receive a Cochrane flock to be driven from Montana—the first big one to be introduced to the Canadian West.

⊳·┤⬥⟩·○·⟨⬥├·⊲

ALEXANDER BEGG HAD A FEW SHEEP at the mouth of the Highwood but they hadn't demonstrated much of anything. It was for the same man who made the bold experiment with cattle in 1881, to put a large flock of sheep to the test and the layout on the Bow River, renamed British American Ranch, seemed like a logical place.

Managing the British American unit was Virginia-born W. D. Kerfoot, six feet tall, erect and broad in the shoulders. Probably his heart was not with sheep but, nevertheless, he was a versatile stockman, having ranched for himself on the Musselshell River in Montana—until prairie fire cleaned him out there. With the Cochrane herd of 1881, he rode onto Canadian soil and fancied what he saw. He was twenty-seven years of age and decided to stay. Kerfoot was a skillful horseman—liked the bad horses as well as the good ones—and usually kept one or more hard bucking horses on hand just for entertainment. One in particular, a chestnut gelding, gained fame by having jolted the conceit out of most itinerant cowboys who tried to ride him.

On July 9, 1884, Kerfoot and the Senator were seen leaving Calgary by team and democrat, setting out for Sun River in Montana for the announced purpose of buying six thousand sheep. Actually they bought eight thousand—far more sheep than existed in the whole of the Northwest Territories up to that time.

Sheep enjoyed no more public affection in Montana than elsewhere in the cattle kingdom and numbers were comparatively small. The few sheepmen, ornery enough to ignore the prevailing resentment, used Merino rams and hence the mutton qualities in their stock left much to be desired. The animals were small and wrinkled in their Merino skins but other characteristics like hardiness and a pronounced tendency to flock or remain together on the range were in their favor.

Cochrane was able to buy the number he wanted at about $3 each and, for the purpose of travel, the big band was divided into two smaller ones. The two flocks would keep about a day's journey apart and each, with several herders, would enjoy such luxury as a camp wagon or sheep wagon would afford. Thus this institution, normally a sheep herder's home on wheels and not to be confused with the cowboy's more glamorous chuckwagon, was introduced to the Canadian range.

Under the ordinary circumstances of solitary occupation, the canvas-roofed sheep wagon was the ultimate in household compaction, combining the essentials of kitchen, dining-room, bedroom and sheepdog quarters—everything except bathroom for which few herders had ever expressed interest—in a single small package. It wasn't likely to fill any feminine heart with envy but it was all the average herder wanted in the way of housekeeping quarters.

Each of the Cochrane wagons on that trail from Sun River to the Bow had extra bunks along with the customary stove, table, cupboard and benches. Two bunks were built crosswise at the rear end and two benches created by extending the caboose structure over the wheels served as cramped seats at meal time and hard beds at night. With four sheep herders sleeping in the tiny quarters, the morning atmosphere was just slightly less turbid than cowboy coffee.

There were the inevitable sheep dogs on the Cochrane drive but nothing exists to indicate the exact number, or where they were obtained.

And with none of the conveniences of corrals in which to pen the sheep secure from predators and Indians at night, one man with loaded rifle remained on guard duty through the spooky hours when the squeak of a field mouse could sound like a Piegan war whoop.

>-·+>-·O-·<+·-<

THE DISTANCE TRAVELLED DAILY was half or less than half as great as that normally made by cattle on the trail—about six miles. There were lambs to be considered and grazing and resting occupied much of the daylight hours. The biggest obstacles to progress were the rivers, and only those who have tried to entice a flock of sheep to cross a stream will understand the magnitude of frustration to be experienced. Forcing cattle into a water crossing was bad enough but with sheep it was trouble compounded. As herders crowded a flock to the river's edge they hoped that some excited members of the timid race would forget their inhibitions and plunge out into the stream and swim away. But, alas, it rarely happened; the crowded sheep at the front of the flock would simply turn their rumps to the water and brace themselves.

It was then for an aggrieved attendant, mumbling words to which sheep herders and ox drivers laid special claim, to make his way through the tightly packed mass of throbbing mutton and force a few of the foremost ewes into the water. But almost invariably, the contrary things would forthwith swim back to the starting point, displaying less fear of man than of water. The idea of civil disobedience almost certainly originated with the genus Ovis.

One trick remained: if the stream was shallow, a sheep could be carried or dragged into the water and held there or, in the event of excessive depth, the selected animal would be led behind a rowboat and thus forced to swim. With exactly the proper timing and urging from the rear of the flock, flustered sheep might take the plunge and follow.

Averaging the six miles a day, exclusive of Sundays when wagons remained stationary, the Cochrane flocks were on the trail for more than two months in that summer. Frank White left Big Hill to meet the incoming sheep and encountered them at Stand-Off at the end of August and remained to assist in forcing them across the Belly River. Calgary people about this time were hearing reports concerning flock progress, reading in the local paper, for example, that "Mr. Kerfoot, superintendent of the Cochrane Sheep Ranch, is homeward bound from Montana with eight thousand sheep."

The big news came a month later when the *Calgary Herald* of September 24th reported: "Mr. Kerfoot of the B.A. Ranche Co., arrived with his band of sheep at the Elbow River on Monday evening. On Tuesday morning they were swam across the river and the novelty of the operation caused a flutter of excitement among the onlookers. The band, which is composed of Merinos and Shropshires and a cross of the two breeds, numbers about eight thousand. They have averaged about six miles per day and come through with scarcely any loss and are as fat as butter. Until Mosquito Creek was reached not one of them was footsore but, having encountered a storm there, a few of them became lame. They will reach the Big Hill this week."

For people in Calgary—the place not yet incorporated as a town—it was the most absorbing event of the season, at least since the installation of a ferry on the Bow River. Though it sounded like sheer heresy to the cattlemen, the *Herald* editor added an expression of his faith that an industry of importance had been given birth. "We are persuaded," he wrote, "that the sheep interest which is just budding will in a few years be the largest and most important in the Territory."

While the sheep were still dripping with water from the Elbow, they were driven to the Bow, treated to the luxury of the new ferry and then turned toward Big Hill, following the same route as that taken by the first herd of Cochrane cattle, exactly three years before. A few weeks later, two hundred rams with proud pedigrees arrived from England. Unloaded from freight cars at Calgary, they, too, were driven to the ranch.

SENATOR COCHRANE WAS AGAIN GIVING LEADERSHIP in a bold way. But it was too much to expect that the pioneer effort would escape reverses. The sheep wintered well—very well—but in the spring, before shearing time, prairie fire raced across the Cochrane range and a part of the flock was caught in the path of the flames. Men who saw the fire approaching tried to move the band but with characteristic lack of co-operation from the sheep, the attempt was too late and the *Macleod Gazette* of April 25, 1885, reported that, "Four hundred of the sheep of the British American Ranch Co., N.W.T., will probably die from being caught by the prairie fire a week ago." And then the news story related what men who understood the old animosities between cattlemen and sheepmen suspected: "Mr. Kerfoot, the manager, says he is satisfied the prairie was set on fire in three distinct places in order to damage the stock."

Actually, the loss was not as high as at first reported; wool is not readily inflammable and most of the severely singed sheep recovered. But spectators who were shocked by the suggestion of criminal intentions on somebody's part, were favorably impressed by the shearing record—fifty thousand pounds of wool to be shipped to the East for sale at Montreal. "That's a lot of wool," people meeting on Calgary's Stephen Avenue agreed. And at the current price of eighteen and one-half cents a pound in Eastern Canada, the clip was worth almost $10,000. Thus from the first crop of wool, the owner received about one-third of the purchase price for the entire flock.

Senator Cochrane—trail blazer, man of imagination and courage—was filled with hope. In 1886, his flock on the British American range numbered an imposing twelve thousand sheep. The success did not go unnoticed and in each of the next few years other flocks were on the trails leading from Montana to new ranges beyond the Highwood and the Bow.

As for Kerfoot who later ranched for himself in Grand Valley, perhaps the sheep were not his first love, but his management of the pioneer flock was good and his counsel about the expanding industry was wise. Nobody could blame him from keeping his warmer affection for his horses—the good ones and the mean ones. Ironically, he met his death when he lost control of a frisky one and was thrown; it was in front of the grandstand at the Dominion Exhibition in Calgary in 1908.

Second Flock of
Collective Cussedness

FRANK WHITE, DAPPER LITTLE MAN FROM CORNWALL, Ontario, was hard on horses. It was inevitable in one who travelled as fast and far at a time when a buckboard offered the ultimate in luxury for the road. But when he drove twenty-five hundred sheep from Choteau, Montana, to Morley beside the Bow River in 1885, he surprised his friends with philosophical restraint such as would do credit to a seasoned shepherd. It was the second big flock brought to what is now the province of Alberta.

White differed in an important respect from most stockmen of his time by keeping a day-to-day record of events whether travelling by wagon or near exhaustion from trying to force a band of perverse sheep across a bridgeless river.

The idea of embarking upon sheep and driving a foundation flock from Montana resulted from his associations with W. D. Kerfoot. Both were employed by the Cochrane interests, White as a treasurer and Kerfoot as manager of the British American ranch. White knew all about balance sheets and ledgers when he came to the West by way of Fort Benton in 1882 but little concerning livestock. That, however, changed quickly and two years later, after seeing the huge Cochrane flock delivered at Big Hill, White was resigning for the purpose of ranching on his own behalf. By this time, he had a place with log cabin and good grass above Ghost River—and he had friends. Richard Hardisty of the Hudson's Bay Company was prepared to invest $5000 in a sheep raising venture such as White had in mind.

➤━◆➤━O━◆━┃━◄

BUT COMPARED WITH THE RICHLY-BACKED Cochrane project, White's resources seemed meagre and he knew that success would depend upon the amount of enterprise and hard work he would devote personally to the plan. As the expedition began on June 27, 1885, it had all the appearance of a one-man effort. White was leaving his log cabin at Morley, driving alone with wagon and two horses—Billy and Dick—going to some undetermined part of Montana.

Perhaps he knew where he would get additional help. As planned, he stopped to spend the first night at the Kerfoot home on the British American ranch and when leaving next morning, two Cochrane men were accompanying. One was Jim Robertson with whom White had earlier discussions about a venture with sheep. He'd go along to Montana and take his Collie pup which might be of some help. The other man was a Cochrane sheep herder, Mike by name, an excellent sheepman as long as he remained on the range and was not confronted by alcoholic temptation. But as time was to prove, Mike possessed an unusual capacity for trouble. Kerfoot agreed that if Mike behaved himself, he would be a most useful helper. And Mike, being half transient, could be ready for the trip on a moment's notice; almost immediately he assembled all his worldly belongings: one horse, two sheep dogs, some not-very-clean blankets and the lanolin-saturated clothes on his back. According to agreement, he would receive food on the way south and $45 a month after sheep were bought.

At Calgary, on the following day, White made some purchases, mainly a tent, small stove and some picket pins for use in tethering the horses at night. The business didn't take long but when ready to start south on the Macleod Trail, Mike was missing. Robertson agreed that they should not go without the herder. A search revealed the awful truth; Mike was in jail. Having found somebody selling bootleg whisky, he had consumed too much and become involved in a fracas on Stephen Avenue.

What was to be done? "We might leave him there," White suggested, "but there are his dogs and horse and we'll need the dogs even though we could get along without Mike."

Before there was time for a decision, Mike appeared at the wagon, obviously in a hurry to be travelling. "If you're not ready to leave," he said, "I will go now and wait for you at Fish Creek."

Mike's hurry to leave town was understandable. Sure, he made a mistake which wasn't uncommon among sheep herders; having imbibed too freely, he undertook to avenge all the indignities against men of his profession. But before he remembered that there was such a thing as police authority, he was in jail and only then did it occur to him that Frank White might be ready to continue the journey. The police guard wouldn't listen to reason and at an opportune moment, Mike, with the strength of a small ox, broke the jail door and walked out. He was now sober enough to know that the police would be coming again to claim him and he wanted to be on the trail.

>─┤◆>─O─<◆├─<

WEATHER WAS GOOD FOR TRAVEL and an aura of peacefulness pervaded the country along the Macleod Trail. Earlier in the season there had been warfare on the South Saskatchewan River, north of Saskatoon, but the insurgents under Louis Riel were beaten and the widespread fear of Indian uprising in sympathy with the Metis cause was vanishing.

White and Robertson conversed about sheep and tried to forget Mike's indiscretions—at least until they camped for a night at Dupuyer Creek in Montana. Again Mike found the bad company for which he had a natural affinity. When it was time to start in the morning, the wayward fellow was missing. When located, Mike was in no condition for the road and to wait would mean delay. White, in no mood for more loss of time, gave Mike the money he had been carrying for him, turned over the horse and dogs which were his property and said "farewell". The inebriated herder was left behind.

"It's too bad," White remarked, "but if we took him to Benton, chances are we'd lose him in that wicked place anyway." What hurt most was the fact of losing Mike's dogs, leaving only Robertson's untutored pup to perform some slight part of the never-ending service an understanding dog can give a shepherd.

Around Fort Benton, White and Robertson saw sheep but prices were high; after ten days they moved up the Teton River to Choteau and on August 5th, bought a band of twenty-five hundred Merinos and an extra team of horses, hired two helpers—one of whom had a dog—and started northward, following foothills where watering places would be plentiful. One man drove the wagon and four-horse team and three men with the help of a green dog and greener pup, kept the sheep moving.

Along the way they took delivery of thirty-eight Merino rams bought at Dupuyer Creek and seemed to be making good time until faced with the crossing of Birch Creek. There the true stubbornness of sheep was reaffirmed. Indians gathered and sat on the grass to enjoy the contest between men and Merinos. Only when the Natives, with promise of a carcass of mutton, became co-operators instead of spectators was success achieved. Men dragged individual ewes into a shallow part of the stream and to the opposite side, holding them until the great mass of sheep broke in bewilderment and followed.

The trouble at Birch Creek was repeated at Two Medicine River, as White's notation for the day shows: "Tried every way we could think of for about four hours when we and the sheep were exhausted—just thinking of giving up until tomorrow when R. drew two old ewes to middle of river; Indians helped carry half a dozen lambs ... and the whole band followed."

At Cutbank River there was more of the same sort of frustration and delay until White hired some people to drag a few rams through the fast-running water. But unexpectedly, the

party forded the South Fork of Milk River with no delay whatever. In approaching that stream there had been an eighteen
mile drive without water and at its end the sheep were naturally
extremely thirsty. When water was sighted, they rushed madly
into the river and the men blocked retreat. The band was
obliged to continue across. It was a trick which wasn't forgotten
when the North Fork had to be crossed but evidently the same
strategy didn't work at the St. Mary River on the Canadian side.
There the sheep were in one of their orneriest moods, determined not to get their nice Merino wool wet. Shouts and curses
from the men and growls from the dogs were ignored by the
stubborn creatures. At nightfall, even after a full day of struggling, the sheep were divided, eight hundred having crossed the
river and the balance of seventeen hundred still on the south
side. White had reason for disgust.

The Belly crossing promised to be better—at least, if
the number of Indians present to "help" was any indication.
But the Natives had ulterior motives; their interest was in
lamb meat more than any lofty principles of co-operation.
They tried to guide the flock over a cutbank, as they succeeded in doing a year later when De Mars from Montana
was bringing a band north. On that occasion, "about one
hundred and seventy sheep were smothered" in the pile-up,
"two or three hours after the sheep had been killed, not a
carcass could be seen, all of them having been carried away
by the Indians."

White managed to avoid such a disaster but didn't prevent
the hungry Bloods from stealing some lambs while making a
pretence of assisting.

It was perfectly plain, however, that the sheep didn't want
to learn anything new. Their conduct at the Oldman and
Highwood was no different than that at the first stream
encountered in Montana. There was just one essential differ-
ence in circumstances at these more northerly rivers: White
was among acquaintances and friends and there was ample help.
Even the celebrated Lord Boyle was among the volunteers at
the Oldman.

Beside the Highwood, two hundred and fifty of the imported sheep were cut out for C. McDonald and placed in Buck Smith's corral.

>─┤◄►─O─◄►┤─◄

IT WAS GOOD TO BE NEARING CALGARY. The place possessed some of the attractions of home for both White and Robertson. White, more conscious than most sheep men would be of a two-month's growth of whiskers and long hair, rode on ahead to engage a barber and announce the flock's early arrival. While the sheep were still five days out, the *Calgary Herald* had news: "Mr. Frank White has just returned from Montana with twenty-five hundred Merino sheep; two hundred and fifty of these have been sold to Mr. C. McDonald, Sheep Creek. The remainder will be driven to Mr. White's ranch near Morley. Mr. White intends placing thoroughbred Merino bucks with his band instead of crossing with the heavier class."

The next river crossing possessed the distinctiveness of familiarity; it was at the I. G. Baker ford on the Elbow— September 21st. And even after the numerous crossings during the journey, this one was no easier than the first one.

Later on that day the sheep were directed to the ferry on the Bow and thus conveyed to the north side. There was still one crossing—at the Ghost—and it took the customary three or four hours of persuasion and toil. But during the night of the next day, White slept in his own cabin at Morley almost exactly three months after leaving the place.

But a sheepman's troubles are never all behind him. Almost at once there was a whispering protest about sheep being allowed into a district where cattlemen thought they had prior rights. As the first winter wore on, the protests grew louder. With Reverend John McDougall raising the most vociferous objection, an independent listener might have concluded that sheep were horrible monsters or carried something like bubonic plague. So acute did the controversy become that Frank White finally moved everything to the south side of the Bow where he founded the well-known Merino ranch. There he ranched for many years, happy that he could have the river's company without having to repeat those crossing tests between human ingenuity and the collective cussedness of twenty-five hundred Merinos.

Thoroughbreds on the Hoot Owl Trail

>⊷⊷⊶⊷⊷⊶⊷⊷⊷⊶⊷⊷<

WHEN TOM LYNCH WHISKED A SMALL GROUP of impounded race horses out of Calgary at a midnight hour and headed for a scheduled foothills trail to Montana, he had no thought of making Thoroughbred history. He was merely trying to help a horseman who found himself the victim of despairing circumstances. But the fact was that in this little herd being snatched from under the nose of the Calgary sheriff was a mare destined through her daughter, May W, to bring fame to the breed. Just about everybody in the racing world at a later date knew about May W, said by the late James Speers to be "the greatest thoroughbred raised in Canada."

High River's Tom Lynch was a fearless fellow—also a foxy fellow with some Robin Hood qualities. In conducting long and dangerous drives with cattle or horses, nobody could compare with him. For years he spent more time on the dusty trails bringing foundation stock for Canadian ranches than on his own place beside the Highwood.

Some of the Lynch undertakings were big like the North West Cattle Company drive from Idaho in 1882. All of them called for courage and skill. And this one involving the debt-ridden Thoroughbreds, though small, possessed the essentials for a good mystery story. Fortunately, William Henry who went to

High River in 1885 and retained a good memory for the many miles he rode with Lynch, was able to recall the circumstances.

><+><+><O><+><+><

LYNCH LOVED A RACE HORSE—loved any good horse—and was always ready to place one of his own fast nags in a contest. Hence he knew all the horsemen who indulged in the sport, knew the Montana man, Reynolds, who brought a string of aristocratic Thoroughbreds to Calgary for some holiday racing in the summer of 1889. Calgarians, even at that period, were ever eager for a race, ready to drop their work at any hour to watch one on the main avenue or on a piece of level ground beside the Elbow River.

But Reynolds had under-estimated the calibre of the Calgary runners. Tom Lynch's Grey Eagle, driven from Oregon with stock for the High River Horse Ranch two years before, was there and too fast for the entries from Montana. Reynolds was not only losing races but he was losing bets and buying horse feed for which he was unable to pay. Sad to say, it was an experience not uncommon among horsemen; debt was mounting steadily, alarmingly. Then, as he might have feared, the local sheriff, with all the brusqueness of the law, seized the string of Thoroughbreds and announced a sale to satisfy the creditors.

Ruing the day he crossed the International Boundary to come to Calgary, Reynolds wished there was a means by which he could steal his beloved Thoroughbreds from the Canadian sheriff and drive them over some little-used trails to Montana and home. A man threatened with the loss of horses to which he was devotedly attached could be pardoned for such alien thoughts. Evidently the idea was shared with an understanding friend who advised in a whisper, "Talk to Tom Lynch. He's your man if you want to move horses—or move anything on its own legs."

In desperation the Montana man sought the tall, grizzled "King of the Cattle Trails" and found him ready to listen. Lynch was a law-biding citizen but in this instance he believed there had been some injustice. Reynolds, he was convinced, was really a decent fellow experiencing a bit of bad luck. He shouldn't be blamed if some of the sharp horsemen about town had contrived to fleece him. Sympathy for people in need was a characteristic by which Billy Henry and other pioneers remembered Tom Lynch.

Whether or not there was any promise of payment for services rendered is not known and never will be known. But Lynch, after listening to the fellow-horseman's story, nodded his willingness to help.

"We better move fast," Tom said. "Start after midnight tonight. If we can get 'em out of town, we'll be all right, I figure. Moonlight these nights. I'll be ready. You be down there at the corral so we'll be sure to get the right horses. It would be hell if we got 'em into Montana and then found we had the wrong ones."

While Calgary was wrapped in the stillness of a foothills night and only a few of Peter Prince's newly-installed arc lights on short poles broke the darkness, a padlock was pried from a corral gate beside Atlantic Avenue and two men moved inside the enclosure.

"We might have trouble getting them across the river at night," Lynch said to Reynolds. "They're Thoroughbreds, you know. You better lead one until we are on the other side of the Elbow, and then I can take care of everything. It won't be long till sunup. All right, let's go."

<hr>

AS MORNING RAYS BEGAN TO SHOW on the eastern sky, Tom Lynch mounted on a favorite big gelding and guiding the uneasy Thoroughbreds, was crossing Fish Creek, a few miles west of Samuel Shaw's woolen mill beside the Macleod Trail. Now he could relax; nothing short of a bloodhound could overtake him from this point on in the sparsely settled country to the southwest. There in the shelter of the cottonwoods of the creek-bed he let the horses graze and rest awhile before moving toward Sheep Creek. He wondered how Reynolds would fare when the sheriff learned what had happened during the night.

Perhaps, with a horseman's sagacity, he too was at that moment travelling south on the Macleod Trail at a fast pace.

At first the Thoroughbreds were difficult to drive. They wanted to turn back to Calgary, but now in the daylight a homing sense seemed to possess them, and they moved with fresh eagerness toward Montana.

Tom Lynch drove his little herd across Sheep Creek at a point close to the Quorn Ranch headquarters and there halted for the night. As the sun was setting, he talked with negro John Ware who was in charge of the Quorn horses and inspected the imported Thoroughbred stallions heading the most ambitious horse breeding enterprise in the West. Together, the two great horsemen then studied each of the animals in the transient band and agreed that a little chestnut mare which Reynolds called Sangaroo was the pick of the lot. She had fine bone, excellent withers and an expressive face. Good breeding was plainly visible.

"She's sho' nice," John Ware said; "Ah think yo'd get somethin' awfu' good from that lady an' ma ol' Plume," referring to the Quorn stallion, Eagle Plume.

Tom Lynch continued on his way westward from the Quorn ranch and then south through foothill country rarely visited by any except Indians. Somebody called it the Hoot Owl Trail. Actually, there was no trail. Nor was there fenced field or corral into which the horses could be placed for security at night. But Lynch, from long experience, had learned how to wrap himself in a blanket and sleep with one eye open to watch his stock.

Though armed with the trusty revolver carried over thousands of trail miles, he didn't have any reason to use it on the trip; this country where foothills met the mountains, he had entirely to himself. Even the International Boundary presented no problems because there was neither an officer nor anything else to mark the place.

After six or seven days of circuitous travel, Lynch and the Thoroughbreds were at a designated point in Montana—near Flathead Lake. Reynolds had not yet arrived but Lynch delivered the horses, and with no more ceremony than would be

expected from a grocer delivering prunes, the man from High
River mounted and turned his horse toward home.

><>·•·○·•·<><

IT WAS JUST ONE MORE in a long list of trailing expeditions for
Tom Lynch but in this instance he was merely trying to help
another horseman. Perhaps reward for these long days in the
saddle and short nights sleeping on the ground had not entered
his mind but recompense did come.

Weeks later, rancher Charlie Knox who lived in the hills
southwest of High River, found a stranger sleeping in his stable
at an early morning hour. In adjacent stalls were two horses, the
man's saddle horse and a strikingly refined chestnut mare.
Upon being questioned, the stranger admitted he had ridden
from Montana to deliver the mare and was instructed to take a
back-country route.

It was quite evident that the stranger was guarding his
answers with care but when leaving the Knox place, he had a
question: "How would I get to Tom Lynch from here?"

The mare brought back in this one-horse drive and delivered to Tom Lynch as a reward for his professional and
unselfish assistance was Sangaroo, the little chestnut John Ware
had admired and Lynch considered the best of the lot. It was a
gift the High River man thoroughly appreciated and in due
course the mare was branded TL and turned out with the rest
of the Lynch horses. Now and then she was brought in and saddled for a race and always she demonstrated her gameness and
Thoroughbred metal.

Tom Lynch loved Sangaroo but he was a horseman and, like
others of the strain, was ready at any time to sell or trade. The
mare was acquired by Duncan Cameron of Calgary and her
name became Froila. Perhaps it was necessary, owing to the
strange circumstances of her entry into Canada to have a new
name. Anyway, when in Cameron's possession, she was bred to
the Quorn horse, Eagle Plume, one of the greatest
Thoroughbred sires ever to be brought to the West. It was the

mating about which John Ware had speculated and in fulfillment of the hope expressed came a bay filly to be named May W.

Tom Lynch died in 1892 and did not see the foal but those who saw her recognized inherited quality, and some thought they could see the promise of speed and greatness. The filly was trained by George Wentworth and when Cameron's racing entries were moved to the United States, May W began to win fame. She loved a race, just like Tom Lynch loved a race, and could be counted upon to give all the effort she possessed. At the end of her first season, May W was proclaimed the outstanding two-year-old of the year.

>─┤◆>─○─<◆├─<

BUT FOR MAY W AS FOR HER STORY-BOOK MOTHER, life was eventful. From a racing stable at Butte, Montana, she was stolen at night and recovered days later at Havre. She figured in a train wreck and emerged unscratched.

Then, Duncan Cameron died and his horses were sold by auction—May W among them. Her purchaser shipped her to England, home of the breed where none but the best were appreciated. There the Alberta-bred bay added steadily to her laurels. There she raced successfully and produced some outstanding offspring. She came to the end of a spectacular Thoroughbred trail at the age of twenty-one years, to be remembered as one of the greatest of her breed in Canada, the United States and England.

It was too bad that Tom Lynch whose skill with horses and cattle—and eagerness to help anybody in trouble—created the dramatic background for the story of May W, did not live to witness the climax.

Hull's Horses

A MASSIVE STEER WEIGHING three thousand, six hundred and fifty-five pounds was paraded slowly down snow-covered Stephen Avenue in Calgary on a December day in 1894. Admiring citizens stood on plank sidewalks while the owner, William Roper Hull, walked behind the animal and waved with natural good humor to his friends. An editor of that day commented that if allowed time, "the steer could have laid on five hundred pounds more."

The purpose of the steer's public appearance was to advertise Hull's beef for the Christmas trade but in a significant sense, the giant ox symbolized the way Roper Hull did everything—in a big way.

As a rancher, horseman and meat dealer, the jovial Hull was consistently successful. Large ranches like the Bow Valley just south of Calgary, Pine Coulee, about fifty miles to the southwest, and Nose Creek spreads were indicative. And in Calgary, Hull was like Pat Burns, ready for any challenge. He built the Grain Exchange Block, Victoria Block, Hull's Opera House, and helped to organize various local industries. All the while, his retail meat operations expanded like a brewmaster's waist-line. Business activities along with Hull philanthropy captured public attention while the gigantic and unparalleled drive of twelve hundred horses from the heart of British

Columbia, bringing the man to Calgary in the first instance, was almost forgotten. In point of both size and obstacles, it was unique.

>·◄►·O·◄►·◄

LIFE FOR ROPER HULL, OF COURSE, was one big adventure after another—and nearly always profitable. Driving the broncho horses out of Kamloops to follow devious inter-mountain valleys to a far-away destination was the sort of challenge the young Englishman accepted unflinchingly. Without such spirit of daring and enterprise he would have remained in Somerset, rejecting the risks associated with life in a new world beyond the Atlantic. But hundreds of times after Calgary became his home, he was heard to say, "By jove, we'll chance it."

Pioneers remembered Roper Hull as a round-faced fellow with cropped black whiskers and sparse hair. He was always cheerful and generous but, being a man of action, he reacted badly to delays and waste of time. Even in church, when the parson preached too long, Roper Hull would squirm in annoyance and chew peppermints at an accelerating rate until the man in the pulpit couldn't fail to get the hint.

In leaving the family home in England in 1873, the 17-year-old and his 18-year-old brother were going to join Uncle Robert Roper who had taken to ranching at Kamloops. To get there they booked passage to Panama, walked across the Isthmus and then continued by sailing ship to the Fraser River. It took months and there was still the most difficult part of the journey—inland to Kamloops—which they did on foot, "in order to save time."

Ranching was in a primitive state. A few people like the uncle were raising and branding cattle and horses but with neither market nor promise of market except for the few head a trail-hardy person might drive to the coast, ranching was more like an unprofitable hobby than a business. But the life suited the young Englishmen like a tea party suits a bachelor minister and on the grassy meadows near the Thompson River the brothers started for themselves, started with fifty horses and a smaller number of cattle.

>—⊱⊰—◦—⊱⊰—⊰<

"GYPSY" JOHNNY WILSON, Lewis "Shifty" Campbell and Thaddeus Harper were their neighbors, all with growing herds. These men surpassed the Hulls in experience but not in enterprise. If anyone with the will and the cash to buy a steer or horse appeared on the scene, Roper Hull would be the first to reach him and make a sale. As construction crews were building the CPR eastward from the Pacific in 1882 and '83, the Hulls had the contract to furnish beef and in that way they were able to dispose of surplus cattle. There was still the problem of finding a market for horses, of which the Hulls now had many. Some were sold for use by the railroad contractors but hundreds remained unbroken and unwanted.

"Too bad the railroad isn't completed," a construction foreman commented. "If those horses were on the Prairies, you'd sell them—every hoof."

"You're sure we could sell them over there?" Hull questioned thoughtfully. "By jove, we can drive them, you know. How far would it be?"

"It's not the distance," the railroad man replied. "There's no direct road—not even a trail. The horses would be dead of old age before you got 'em to Macleod or Calgary. You'll just have to wait till we finish this railroad and then you can ship."

But with typical impatience, Roper Hull said that would be too long to wait. He had horses to sell and was determined to act. The brothers were in British Columbia ten years when the big drive was undertaken. Neither had ever seen the prairie side of the mountains and neither had more than a vague idea of how to get there.

"But we might as well chance it," said Roper Hull. "If we don't get through, we won't lose much anyway. Horses are no good if you can't sell them. Between us we've got close to three hundred so let's get them together."

The horse round-up began. Between the three Hulls there were fully as many horses as Roper had estimated but, as other stockmen along the Thompson River learned of the plan, they pleaded that some of their horse stock be included. If the animals could be sold in the Territories beyond the Selkirks and Rockies, they'd accept any settlement, the neighboring owners assured.

The foolhardy undertaking was Roper Hull's idea in the first place and he was making the plans. "Sure thing, you can throw your bunch in with ours," he told one horseman and then another and another. Pretty soon the horse herd numbered six hundred, then eight hundred and, when the drive was started away from the river in the late summer of 1883, it included twelve hundred head. The animals were of many sizes and colors but possessed one characteristic in common, a wildness imparted by life in a mountainous terrain.

The task of controlling and guiding such a mass of equine self-will over unfamiliar trails was enough to frighten most men. But if the Hull boys felt alarm, they were not displaying the symptoms and their uncle, while advising to keep their guns handy and stay in open country as far as possible, bade them good luck.

>-◄►-●-◄►-►◄

FOR THE BEGINNING OF THE TRIP, there were extra helpers—at least twenty mounted men, most of whom intended to ride only until the band accepted the necessity of being driven. The first day was trying and exhausting, as horses with wild spirits tried to turn back to home pastures. On reaching Grand Prairie, saddle horses were exhausted. The only good feature was that all the horses were tired and holding them during the first night presented less than anticipated difficulty.

Weary men ate their suppers beside the supply wagons and those not assigned to the dreary night-watch bedded down with such shelter as the branches of pine trees would afford. Thus they would live—often tired, often hungry, often wet—for weeks. But complaint was unfashionable.

On the second day, horsemen saw the Okanagan Lake and pressed southward toward the Mission and Osoyoos. Thus far the Hulls were familiar with the country but beyond the south end of the lake, they would be total strangers to the trail and the obstacles it would present.

The Okanagan Trail had been pounded by big herds on other occasions and was clearly marked. Now and then for a decade, cattle had been driven south as well as north but this was the first band of horses to be moved across the border, southward and, indeed, the biggest horse herd to travel in either direction.

There was temptation to turn eastward at Osoyoos and try to follow the International Boundary to the Prairies but Lewis Campbell, who knew everything about trails, cautioned to "go deep into the States before swinging east or you'll find yourselves cut off by mountains and lakes."

The temporary riders turned back as soon as the drive was assuming an order of routine. Horses seemed able to make eighteen or twenty miles a day and still get enough grazing to satisfy appetites. About the only delays were occasioned by late-foaling mares and arguments with settlers in the State of Washington, who wondered if some of their horses had been attracted by the herd and were in danger of being swept away to Calgary.

Even at Tonasket, well below the Boundary, the decision about an easterly course had not been made. Men along the way repeated the warning, "Stay well to the south." They continued south to the Columbia River and after swimming it, began to bear eastward, finally driving the big band right through Spokane and heading towards Bonner's Ferry and the Canadian border.

>—•◇•—○—•◇•—<

OFTEN THERE WERE WILD RIVERS to swim and again and again the mountains closed in on them but they wound their way back to British Columbia and into the Crow's Nest Pass. There was scarcely any settlement and, in places, not much grass.

But after more days and weeks, the mountains were behind and men and horses faced great expanses of treeless grassland with only a few cattle—mostly with the Stewart Ranch brand—in sight. Cochrane cattle had recently been moved from the Bow River to grass east of Waterton lakes and the first Walrond cattle might have been seen in the hills to the left. No stockman could overlook the opportunities presented by the scene.

Mounted Police on patrol intercepted the horsemen and asked routine questions. The Hulls admitted they didn't know where they were going—just wanted to sell horses. "You might sell some at the Fort," said a man in uniform. "It's just twenty miles ahead."

The horse band was held to graze on the south side of the Oldman while Roper Hull talked to the officials at Fort Macleod. Yes, they wanted horses and asked to see the stock. That afternoon they rode through the band and pointed out the horses they'd buy. There was no argument about price but police needs were limited and the forty or fifty head sold to the force, and one hundred to a private buyer made but little impression upon the big herd, but the sales brought encouragement and the men at Macleod suggested that Fred Stimson of the recently organized North West Cattle Company should be seen.

The transient herd was turned north toward Calgary and at the Highwood River, Fred Stimson was present. Just as the Fort Macleod men had postulated, he bought all the remaining horses. The biggest horse drive in Canadian history was now ended and the Hulls, tired but satisfied, paid off their helpers, sold their cook wagon and rode on to see the shapeless community built about Fort Calgary. The railroad reached the place just a few months earlier and now there was talk of seeking incorporation as a town.

Roper Hull was impressed. "By jove," he told his brother, "this is the place for me. A man could ranch in those hills and do a butcher business in town. I'm coming back."

NEXT YEAR, 1884, ROPER HULL RETURNED to stay and launch a combined ranching and meat business. The first lease was southwest of Nanton and three thousand British Columbia cattle and five hundred horses were shipped to stock it. Operations from that point on were greater and greater, and at one time Roper Hull was the largest owner of real estate in Calgary. But nothing in a varied and successful career had called for more sheer pluck than starting from Kamloops with twelve hundred inter-mountain cayuses to drive six hundred or seven hundred miles over strange and hazardous trails to the Prairies.

Eighteen Thousand Sheep

ANNOUNCING THE SHEEP SENSATION OF THE YEAR, the *Macleod Gazette* of September 26, 1889, reported: "Eighteen thousand sheep arrived at Maple Creek last week from Oregon. They are for Sir John Lister Kaye."

Estimates of the number differed somewhat but whether the total was eighteen thousand or ten thousand, the flock was the first seen in the region of Cypress Hills and the biggest to be brought to the North West Territories. At once the Territorial sheep population was practically doubled.

The drive out of Oregon, across Idaho and Montana and into Canada was started when lambing and shearing were completed, and took all summer. In charge were the seasoned William Riddle and James Ross, porridge-eaters whose skill with sheep matched their Scottish silence.

According to one who saw the mighty band approaching Maple Creek at its own slow rate of travel, the bleating was continuous and sheep covered the landscape like a migrating herd of buffalo such as was seen rather commonly until a decade earlier. The scene seemed to present thousands of heads and ears surfacing on a sea of wool. As for the new town of Maple Creek, it was suddenly overrun with sheep. And Cree Indians who had never seen specimens of the race before, were struck with awe.

>━I━◆>━O━<◆━I━<

BEHIND THE PROJECT WAS SIR JOHN LISTER KAYE, dynamic little Englishman with oversized ideas about farming and ranching. If anyone was born for distinction, it was Sir John. Coming to the western frontier in the 1880s he organized the most spectacular farming and ranching enterprises, created the most sensational agricultural news, made the biggest mistakes and laid indisputable claim to the largest flock of sheep to be driven across the International Boundary—perhaps any International Boundary.

His association with the West was not long but, while it lasted, his big schemes, his milk pails on beef ranches and watering carts on wheat farms entertained prairie spectators and, at the same time, exasperated the men who worked for him.

Sir John won the attention of people in the homestead country in 1885 when, in association with Lord Queensbury, he was embarking upon a seven thousand acre farming scheme at Balgonie. But the man had bigger ideas and in 1887, while thirty plows were breaking ground on the Balgonie place, he was creating the Canadian Agricultural, Coal and Colonization Company to conduct farming and ranching on ten properties of ten thousand acres each, scattered along the new railway as far west as Langdon. Half the land was obtained from the Canadian government and half from the Canadian Pacific Railway. Sir John had no difficulty in securing the necessary British capital.

One of the principal ideas was to bring settlers from the Old Country and establish them on small farms carved from the big expanses of company land, each small place to be fenced, stocked with cattle and provided with not less than twenty acres of cultivation. That much of the land was in the dry belt and unsuited to small farming operations, Sir John refused to admit. He'd make wheat grow there, even if he had to haul water to moisten the arid soil.

What followed was a spending spree such as the homestead country had not witnessed. Sir John gave instructions for the purchase of five hundred Clydesdale mares in Ontario; that number would allow fifty for working and breeding purposes on each of the ten places. Next, he was ordering two million feet of lumber for the construction of buildings. Such was the scale on which he would operate.

Early in the summer of 1888, horses and walking plows were put to work at breaking and preparing the prairie sod for wheat seed. But before the cultivation was far advanced, Sir John decided to develop ranching rather more than grain growing and entered into negotiations with the Powder River Ranch Company for its entire Canadian herd of cattle. That company, with very large cattle interests in Wyoming, bought the Trollinger place on Mosquito Creek a year or so before and trailed six thousand cattle into Canada. Sir John, with characteristic fondness for round numbers and big ones, announced his intention to buy ten thousand cattle—a thousand for each of his ten places—but the seven thousand Powder River cattle then available would be a beginning, he figured, and late in the season, the imported herd was moving again, this time mainly eastward to Sir John's ranches extending across Assiniboia. With the cattle came the famous "76" brand and before long, the new company was becoming known most widely as "The 76."

><+>•O•<+><

NEXT, SIR JOHN TALKED ABOUT getting fifty thousand sheep, that being an impressive figure, one to make everybody take notice. To obtain that many or even half that many, buyers would have to travel far—and company men did indeed travel far. They found sheep for sale in Montana but not enough for their purpose. They went on into neighboring states. Buying and driving began in the State of Oregon, and additional sheep were purchased in Idaho and Montana and added to the band. It seems that just about all the sheep available along the way were bought and taken on the trail pointing to the North and East. The flock, growing steadily bigger, was allowed to travel at little more than voluntary speed. The average progress was not above six miles per day.

The sheep were nearly all of Merino breeding, hence hardy and good travellers. The herders were adequately supplied with dogs and had the usual camp wagon serving as dining room and bedroom on wheels.

Meanwhile, Sir John was continuing to make history of a kind on the Canadian ranches. The season was dry—even drier than usual—and, impulsively, he ordered forty-four wagon-mounted pine tanks with which to haul water from sloughs and wells to irrigate the wheat fields. Had he stopped to calculate that even one inch of water per acre would weigh over a hundred tons, he would have realized the hopelessness of his methods in overcoming drought on his thousand-acre fields. In the first place, there wasn't enough water available to make more than an impression on the big fields. What his men succeeded in hauling, only settled some dust on a few acres. The wheat was still a failure.

But Sir John wasn't self conscious or easily embarrassed by errors. While the sheep were travelling northward, he was ordering consolidation of the cattle at Swift Current Creek and instructing his men to milk some of the cows. Needless to say, the idea was repulsive to the old cowboys who looked with scorn upon anything related to the occupation of dairying, just as it was repulsive to every self-respecting range cow. But orders are orders, and long chutes were constructed into which the hostile cows were driven for the daily struggles at milking times. Protesting cows kicked violently at the disgusting touch of human hands and refused to let down their milk. The result would inspire neither a true dairyman nor an old cowpoke.

Sir John, ever in a hurry, built a creamery in Swift Current and offered a handsome silver trophy to the ranch manager who could report the largest number of cows being milked "by October." But understandably, neither the cows—many of which retained Texas longhorn characteristics—nor the ranch hands co-operated in making the creamery a success. The scheme produced more amusement than butter. With disappointments in both wheat and dairying, the incoming sheep appeared in an ever more attractive light.

THE END OF AUGUST found the immigrant flock crossing from Montana into the North West Territories at a point south of the Cypress Hills. Bewildered Mounted Police, acting as Customs Officers, tried to confirm the declared numbers by making their own counts. But the task of counting more than ten thousand sheep proved altogether too much, even for men who had often practised the art as a cure for insomnia. After getting up to six thousand a couple of times and then losing count, the Mounties gave up, satisfied to accept the herders' word for the number.

The trail over the Cypress Hills went by Fort Walsh, the North West Mounted Police post established in 1875. The ruts were clearly marked by freight wagons and carts travelling between Fort Walsh and Fort Benton. On long drives, herders liked to use the established trails as guides without actually keeping their sheep on them. Often the freshest grazing was away from the trails.

The Cypress Hills in their autumn colors were enough to inspire even the most unemotional sheepherder. Michael Oxarart's horses and a few cattle running there had made but little impression upon the grass resources. Here was more grass than the herders had seen on their entire trip, and the sheep ate until they appeared bloated. There in the Hills, Sir John Lister Kaye met his men and inspected his sheep. He was pleased and enthusiastic. Now, he was sure, the sheep were his brightest hope for ranching success. "We'll fill these Territories with sheep in a few years," he proclaimed.

William Rutherford who had been named sheep manager for "The 76" was at Maple Creek to see the band arrive and formally receive it. He agreed that the sheep were in good condition in spite of the great distance they had travelled—eight hundred miles for some of them—to say nothing of the rivers and other obstacles which had to be faced. Policy, as far as possible, had been to follow streams instead of crossing them.

Maple Creek was the end of the trail but not the end of the journey. There, under Rutherford's supervision, the sheep were divided into ten flocks of about equal size and loaded on freight cars for delivery at the various ranch points. About the same time, imported Cheviot rams arrived and Sir John began to speculate publicly about the number of lams he'd have in the next spring. But regardless of the generation not yet conceived, he had the biggest sheep enterprise in all of Canada.

Before the next year was ended, the idea of keeping the sheep in ten ranch flocks was seen as a mistake and the bands were brought together at Swift Current, Kincorth and Gull Lake. But this time the company inventory showed six thousand four hundred forty-six cattle and about twenty-five thousand sheep.

When Scottish John Omen entered the company's service in 1892, there were thirty thousand sheep, "including wethers." There had been a further shift in administrative policy: operations were now directed from a chain of fifteen camps scattered along a fifty-mile stretch of prairie—two thousand sheep per camp. Shepherds were paid $30 a month with a food-allowance of $12 and a bonus of two bottles of Hudson's Bay whisky at Christmas time. Much of the sale stock from the flocks was now being shipped to England. It was one man's opinion that at least twenty-five thousand company sheep—mostly yearly wethers— were exported to the Old Country by Sir John's company.

>-+-+>-+-O-+-<+-+-<

THE YEAR 1893 WITNESSED what was known as the Great Sheep Depression. Both Canada and United States felt it severely. Good wethers were sold for two cents a pound and buyers were indifferent at any price. Before there was complete economic recovery, Sir John retired and D. H. Andrews went to England where he effected a reorganization. The company took a revised name but to the people on the plains it was still "The 76", still a colorful rangeland enterprise with a better record with sheep than with cattle or wheat or pigs. It was still the company responsible for trailing the biggest single flock of sheep to Canadian soil.

Trail to the Yukon

GOLD IN THE KLONDIKE! Strikes on Bonanza and Eldorado Creeks! The electrifying reports of discoveries in Canada's remote North triggered the maddest gold rush in world history. Nearly forty thousand gold seekers, leaving the security and comforts of civilization behind them, threaded their way over the uncertain northern routes during 1897 and '98, and every one took a vigorous appetite with him.

The inhospitable Yukon could contribute fish and wild game but not nearly enough for the thousands of men and few women who converged recklessly upon Dawson City where the Klondike River joined the Yukon. Marmalade was not their food; they wanted meats and until western stockmen with the courage of Arctic explorers performed the nigh-impossible feat of delivering beef and mutton, famine was an ever-present threat. Even an easily-freighted staple like flour, brought in on the backs of Jack Dalton's pack horses, sold for a dollar a pound. The first cows at Dawson City, eating hay worth $300 or more a ton, rewarded their owners with milk which sold at $3 a quart and butter at $10 a pound—payable in gold dust. Alexander Anderson who accompanied a herd of Pat Burns cattle in 1898 and remained through the winter, told of buying a special treat for his Christmas dinner, three potatoes at a dollar each.

Restaurant meal prices varied according to the bulk of food consumed. A Dawson City hotel announced "Common feed,

$1; square meal, $2; belt-buster, $3; mortal gorge, $4." It may have been the same place of public accommodation which offered: "Good bunks, $2 a night; clean sheets a dollar extra."

>─┤─◆>─•─O─◄•┤─◄

MUSHROOM-LIKE DAWSON EMERGED as a rip-roaring shack-town. Six months after the first cabin was erected, the place could boast five hundred structures—mostly log—including a few hotels, several dance halls and at least a score of saloons. An offer to exchange a gold mine on Bonanza Creek for one of the popular saloons was promptly refused by the owner who knew the high earning-power of his establishment.

Mounted police were present to impose a check upon law-lessness but drinking and free spending were as prevalent as in any of the brash cow-towns of the western frontier. Every known form of gambling had its adherents, and the gold dust stakes were big. Such a place could be expected to invite char-acters with all the degrees of respectability—women as well as men. Understandably, citizens loving the conventional ways of life were not attracted.

Ranching of western Canada's prairie, foothill and inter-mountain ranges was just two or three decades old when the rush began and the first stories were told about reward awaiting those cattlemen with the resourcefulness and stamina to take herds over the myriad obstacles in an unmapped hinterland, and deliver fresh meat. Cattle on the ranges had multiplied faster than market demands, and ranchers selling fat steers for three cents a pound listened eagerly to the reports about dollar-a-pound beef at faraway Dawson City. But how was beef pro-duced at Brandon, Moose Jaw, Medicine Hat and Calgary to be transported to that distant place? Who would have the nerve or foolhardiness to try it?

For the miners going into the Yukon gold fields there were four or more possible routes—all difficult and dangerous. There was the overland route from Edmonton, cursed by all who attempted it. A second route, appearing falsely to offer advantages, led overland through Northern British Columbia. Another was upstream on the Yukon River, beginning at the Bering Sea and looping over the Arctic Circle; even on the map it appeared tough, and not many people went that way. And, finally, there was the five hundred or six hundred-mile land and water course inland from Skagway, chosen by the great majority of miners.

Exactly the same alternatives faced those cattlemen bold enough to consider an expedition which would be bad enough without the constant encumbrance of a herd of ornery steers.

Edmonton businessmen did all possible to induce miners to buy their blankets, guns, axes, flour and gold pans on Jasper Avenue and begin the thousand-mile endurance journey from there. And not to be outdone, Calgarians tried to make a case for starting from their foothills city, advertising the advantages in glowing terms: "Calgary Overland Route To Yukon—the only all-Canadian route via Edmonton, Peace and Pelly rivers. Good feed, timber and game. Gold prospects all the way. Climate temperate, suitable in many places for agriculture. The City of Calgary is on the main line of the CPR. Horses, cattle and provisions can be bought at lowest prices. Miners' licences issued at Calgary. For further information apply to City Clerk Calgary."

The truth was that few if any miners got through in a northwesterly dash from Edmonton. Most of them saw their horses die along the way, leaving men stranded far from both starting point and destination.

>−◆>−○−<◆−<

OF COURSE, ROGUES AND CONFIDENCE MEN PROSPERED; unsuspecting adventurers were deluged with advice from silver-tongued crooks. Some of the would-be miners, like R. J. Crawford, fresh from Ireland, made their first mistake before leaving Montreal by purchasing $500 tickets on the "Ice Train with heated cars and soft beds," supposed to convey passengers from Edmonton right to Dawson City. Finding the high-priced ticket to be useless because the luxury train to run on ice didn't exist, Crawford went on to Vancouver and Skagway and had the distinction of taking the first two horses over the Chilkoot Pass through to Dawson City where he was able to make $300 a day by hauling logs out of the river for men wishing to use them in house construction.

Nobody could think well of the long, up-stream entry to the gold fields from the mouth of the Yukon River and consequently, practical considerations reduced the routes to two: overland from British Columbia and the one ultimately called the "Trail of '98," from wild and lawless Skagway where men were known to have been shot for the reward of gold fillings in their teeth.

Cattlemen considered the challenge and the dollar-a-pound return if they were lucky. Shipping fresh meat from Medicine Hat or Calgary or even Vancouver was out of the question and slaughtering at Skagway would present the same sort of preservation problems because there would still be the long inland haul by means of pack-train, sled or boat—all without refrigeration. Winter travel would be especially slow and summer temperatures would quickly convert fresh meat to a putrifying mess. There was only one practical method and cattlemen were wise enough to recognize it—take live cattle all the way or nearly all the way before slaughter. As they anticipated, the plan which did succeed consisted of shipping the cattle by rail to Vancouver, ocean-going vessel from there to Skagway or nearby Pyramid Harbour, and over the mountain passes on foot.

At best, it was no expedition for men of faint heart or men who were in a hurry. Nobody taking cattle to Dawson returned in less than six months—and a few never returned.

The first cattlemen over the more direct passes encountered hardships at every turn but ere long, they adopted the Dalton Trail and slaughtered beside the Lewes River—about opposite the mouth of the Pelly and some distance below Rink Rapids. This way they avoided the major rapids between the mountains and Dawson City.

Inasmuch as the first cattle were taken over the Chilkoot Pass, those men in charge were confronted with the same dangers as those which faced the miners—and many more. Some people said the first forty miles from Skagway were the worst but that depended upon whether one ran the wicked rapids lower down or portaged. In any case, it was eight or ten miles from the head of the inlet to the foot of the canyon from which point the Chilkoot Trail became narrower and more treacherous. At some seasons there was the threat of ice and cascading snow; at others, there were mountain streams and falling boulders about which to worry.

>——·⟡·—·O·—·⟡·—<

R. J. CRAWFORD AND HIS TEAM of history-making horses were at Sheep Camp near the foot of the ascent when the frightful avalanche of snow and rocks came down the mountainside in '98, burying tents and taking the lives of sixty-five people and many horses. Instead of crushing Crawford's tent, the snow broke the ropes, took the canvass and left the young fellow with an Irishman's luck and his horse, uninjured.

Snow on 6700-foot Mount Cormack, on the westerly side of the pass, was unpredictable at the best of times.

Nobody knew how many horses died on the first forty miles toward Dawson City—probably most of those taken to Skagway by the miners. Revolting as the thought must be, an observant prospector estimated three thousand rotting carcasses in evidence at one time.

Beyond the summit—some three thousand feet higher than Skagway—a traveller's progress was likely to be faster but no less dangerous. The trail led past Lake Lindeman to Lake Bennett, considered the head of navigation on the chain of lakes and streams by which a miner, with luck, might float all the remaining distance to Dawson City.

Beyond Lake Bennett were Lakes Nares, Tagish and Marsh, separated only by land constrictions. It could be argued that here was one irregular lake rather than three but nobody cared about such technicalities.

Twenty-five miles or so beyond Marsh, the novice sailors on strange and monstrous river crafts, faced the most terrifying portion of the entire route—Miles Canyon and White Horse Rapids. Cautious people elected to unload and portage at that place, and a well-worn path was made around the west side of the troubled waters. Nevertheless, there were those fearless souls, anxious to be spared the extra work and delay represented by a four-mile detour, who took the risk and committed their fortunes and lives to the hellish current.

It was an experience no man could forget. As rafts and cargos shot forward, the river's roar grew louder. The canyon became narrower, its basaltic walls overhanging menacingly. But the gravest dangers created by seething water were still half a mile ahead. It was like being rushed straight to destruction but once in the rapids there was no turning back—any more than for the man who jumps off a bridge. A small boat or raft would be tossed like a cork in a washing machine, resisting all human effort to control it.

>—<>—O—<>—<

NOR WAS THE MAD WHITE HORSE WATER the end of trouble for those clinging to river travel. There was the slow water of Lake Labarge and the rapids at Five Fingers and Rink. There were submerged rocks and the uncertainty in northern weather. The lake water was too slow and the rapids were too fast. The collective dangers and difficulties accompanying those first trips with cattle over the all-water course from Lake Bennett to Dawson led cattlemen to seek alternatives and they adopted the longer Dalton Trail—nearly five hundred miles through subalpine forests, waste lands, rocks and tundra—and the last hundred miles or so by river.

Over the Trail of
Rotting Horse Meat

THE FIRST BEEF-ON-THE-HOOF seen at Dawson City was taken over the rock-strewn trails and down treacherous streams in the late summer of 1897, about a year after the momentous strikes on Klondike River and its tributaries. But whence did the cattle come and who drove them to Dawson? Was the ruffian Jack Dalton, driving thirty Oregon cattle, or William Thorpe from Seattle the pioneer hero and trail blazer as suggested? Were Waechter and Sons from Union Town, Washington, entitled to the honor? Or was an unpretentious Canadian, Edward Fearon from Maple Creek the one who first reached the goal to sell a large quantity of beef at Dawson City for the reward of a dollar a pound or more?

Canadians were slow to claim driving distinctions but on some trails like those leading inland from Skagway, Alaska, their performance called for the historian's highest admiration. Ed Fearon, driving one hundred steers and a family cow, left Skagway at the same time as certain United States cattlemen but there is reason to conclude that he was the first into Dawson City, "the first to take cattle into that region," said the Parliamentary Guide of 1898.

Most people on the prairie and foothill ranges didn't even know he was away until they read in the *Macleod Gazette* of January 21, 1898, "It is reported that Ed Fearon of Maple

Creek who left last summer with a band of cattle for Klondike, got his cattle into the country and disposed of them at high prices. The NWMP bought ten thousand pounds at $1 a pound. The balance was sold at $1.50 per pound."

>─◦─◦─◦─◦─<

FEARON'S LIFE DEMANDED VARIETY like a mangy steer needed a rubbing post. Born in England in 1858, the robust fellow of medium height and dark complexion was successively soldier, mounted policeman, school teacher, politician, rancher and hotel operator. Leaving the School of Gunnery at Kingston in the spring of 1878, he joined the North West Mounted Police and remained with the force until July 31, 1880, when he was discharged at Fort Walsh on his own request. Later, during the rebellion trouble of 1885, Fearon served with Colonel Otter's Scouts and was awarded a medal for bravery.

On October 31, 1894, Fearon was elected to the Legislative Assembly of the North West Territories for the Constituency of Medicine Hat but for much of his term of office he was absent in the North and missed two legislative sessions.

In choosing to live at Maple Creek, he wanted to be in the cattle business and after returning from the Klondike, he ran a Maple Creek hotel. The latter was a husband-and-wife proposition: "she looks after the beds," Fearon explained, "and I handle the pots." But even before he was actively engaged in hotel operation, the saltiest of Maple Creek's citizens and ranchers met at that place to exchange opinions about Frederick Haultain's Territorial Government, discuss the cattle situation and play a little poker. For news of the ranching country, they depended upon the columns of the *Macleod Gazette* and there in the hotel lobby somebody read aloud from the issue of March 26, 1897, "The first beefsteak that ever reached Circle City, Alaska, sold for $48 per pound a few weeks ago. The steaks consisted of a ten-pound piece of beef slaughtered at Forty-Mile Creek, packed and shipped two hundred and fifty miles to Circle City by Thomas O'Brien. When O'Brien reached camp, the miners turned out in a body to see the steak. It was placed on exhibition and attracted as much attention as an eight-legged calf …"

>–+◆>–O–<◆+–<

CATTLE INTRODUCED TO THE CYPRESS HILLS and surrounding plains some ten years before were now quite numerous. Mitchell cattle from Elk Island were often seen at Maple Creek, and Dickson Brothers, who started in 1886 with cattle shipped from Ontario, now had a big herd. But most conspicuous at that time were the "V" cattle, property of Conrad and Price whose ranch headquarters were north of the town. Saucy looking critters with Texas character in their horns and the "V" brand on ribs, they sometimes grazed within the town limits and invited feminine wrath by drinking up the precious soft water from poorly-guarded rain barrels.

"By gosh," Fearon remarked one day after reading the *Gazette*, "There's a powerful rush shaping up for the Klondike River—wherever it is. S'ppose a fellow could get some of these Maple Creek steers to that place and sell them for the big money?"

Among the squatters in the hotel lobby there were conflicting opinions. "You'd never get through," one man insisted, pausing only for a bull's eye shot at the spitoon. "You could ship to Vancouver and up the coast to Alaska, no doubt, but then there'd be mountains a mile high like in B.C. Hell, you'd never get wild cattle over them. Imagine how silly a man'd feel sitting beside those Alaska glaciers with cattle he couldn't move any farther and couldn't sell. You'd better forget it."

"Not so sure about that," Fearon replied. "Aren't the prospectors going over on foot? I'd bet a good man would make it with cattle. Look at this map. There's a river. If a fellow could get to its headwaters, he could make a raft for cattle or drive them along the river. Don't be too sure it can't be done. A man would do a hell of a lot for the joy of selling beef at a dollar a pound or more."

"If you need more steers than you have now, take a cut of my 'V' critters if you want to try it," Fearon heard the Conrad and Price manager offer. "Pay me $45 a head when you get back—and if you don't get back alive, I'll take your cows. Fair enough?"

Fearon knew there could be no success unless the long journey was completed before the cold autumn weather set in. His decision was to go—at once. In a matter of days, saddle horses, pack horses, feed, ropes, guns, bedding, tents, axes and one hundred heavy four-year-old steers were assembled at "The Creek," ready for loading.

"Better take Bessie along," a neighbor suggested, referring to the family milk cow. "She always likes to be in front of a herd and you might need a good leader." Fearon recognized advantage in the proposal, and the brindle cow was loaded along with the steers to fill five stock cars. Horses and equipment filled a sixth.

Sceptical townsmen shook their heads in wonder as Fearon waved farewell from the top of a freight car. "Chances are we'll never see him again," they commented. "Too bad; he was such a good fellow."

THROUGH THE OFFICES of the Canadian Pacific Railway a big scow—like a floating corral—awaited the cattle at Vancouver. When animals and tons of hay were transferred, a tug-boat pulled it northward at a speed which seemed about half as fast as a man would walk.

After many monotonous days during which the men had nothing to do except throw hay to the cattle, the outfit arrived at Skagway, with no losses. There the cattle were held on their scows until preparations were completed for the great adventure over the Pass.

Skagway, well furnished with saloons and overrun by amateur miners and professional gamblers, had all the stir of a circus. Ostensibly, local authority was in the hands of the United States marshal but emerging as the strong-man of the town was a captivating newcomer, trim-waisted, black-bearded, 37-year-old Jefferson Randolph Smith, better known as "Soapy." "If your boys have any money on 'em" a prospector whispered to Fearon, "keep 'em away from that fellow. He'd steal the very gold in their teeth."

The soft-spoken young man with the benign manner of a parson was really wise in the ways of sin. His first play for public attention was a dramatic declaration for justice. There had been a cold-blooded murder and men of Skagway were taking steps to hang the murderer when Soapy Smith with cocked guns intervened and, in high moral tones, condemned mob violence. He'd hate to do it but he'd shoot anybody who departed from the ways of justice. The crowd, impressed, at once agreed that this man should take charge of the town.

Surrounding himself with professional thugs, Soapy did indeed take charge, robbed the prospectors on their way to Dawson City, robbed them of their gold-dust when they came out, and grew rich until that day in 1898 when he was confronted by a posse of irate citizens led by Frank Reid. As Smith and Reid faced each other, they fired simultaneously and, with equally expert marksmanship, both men fell, both mortally wounded.

Fearon was in a hurry to start over the mountains and had no time for Soapy anyway. First there was the problem of transporting hay over the Pass to Lake Bennett. They called it fifty miles; it wasn't that far but it seemed no less. Many of the miners were going over the shorter Chilkoot Pass but the White Pass at twenty-nine hundred feet altitude appeared better for cattle and horses. At that, it was difficult enough for any class of stock and before the end of 1898, it was known as the "Trail of Rotting Horse Meat."

>─┼─◆─○─◆─┼─<

DEPOSITING HAY WAS A HUGE TASK in itself and pack horses went over the route again and again, some meeting death along the way. The first of Fearon's men to reach Bennett, beyond the Pass, remained to construct rafts on which to carry the stock and hay. Two United States cattlemen were at Skagway at the same time, making the same sort of plans and the three herds were ready for the trail simultaneously.

For a few miles out of Skagway there was level trail through spruce forest and then the long climb to the summit. Here the old family cow with pronounced ambition for leadership, proved her worth. She didn't require prodding; with guidance she set out boldly and the steers followed. Even at the summit, Bessie was out in front, and with feminine intuition avoiding the rocky pitfalls more expertly than her emasculated herd-mates.

There were accidents. Steers with broken legs were shot. One critter walked blindly over a precipice and met instant death. Others departed from the trail and were brought back with difficulty. But after a week of hardship, men and cattle arrived at Bennett where scows were almost ready for loading.

Two big rafts and a small one were loaded and the little armada drifted slowly away from the shore. Not sure of what tests lay ahead, men hoped the worst was over. Slow rate of speed was their first worry but where the channel narrowed, the rafts moved briskly. When an expanse of grass was seen, Fearon would order a halt for a day or two of grazing. It was important to save the hay and grain feed as much as possible because he knew that feed shortage would make it necessary to slaughter the cattle—and invite the risk of meat spoiling before reaching Dawson.

Small lakes and connecting streams were left behind and then there was the terrifying experience of White Horse Rapids. Even before realizing the extent of danger, the men were into the rapids and turning back was impossible. They might have encountered destruction but, fortunately, the rafts rode through without mishap. In the wild twisting and tossing, a couple of steers fell over the railing but they were the only losses.

Nights were becoming colder and ice was forming, but the current—except while passing Lake LaBarge—was better for rafting and at the middle of October, Maple Creek's Ed Fearon arrived at Dawson City and slaughtered the cattle under the attentive and hungry gaze of hundreds of miners. They were the first cattle to arrive and the beef met rewarding sale at a dollar a pound and more. Even hides and viscera brought more for dog feed than the best beef was worth at Maple Creek. And Bessie, soon due to calve, was wanted by somebody for a milk cow and sold for a thousand dollars.

>⊷⊶⊙⊷⊶⊰

AFTER COLLECTING PAYMENT IN GOLD-DUST, Fearon settled with his men and made his way back to Skagway, Vancouver and home. For the manager of the V Ranch, he had settlement and for citizens who congregated for politics and poker he had some rich new stories of adventure.

When the old Mountie, rancher and cattle-driver died in 1933, death marked the end of a fifty-year association with Maple Creek.

Bill Henry on the
Dalton Trail

WHEN 92-YEAR-OLD WILLIAM HENRY of High River was
told that he and certain other distinguished pioneers were
to be presented to the Queen and Prince Philip on the
occasion of the Royal Visit at Calgary in 1959, the little
man with the Scottish accent and laudable economy in the
use of words, said, "I have no time for that kind of thing."
But friends insisted that he attend and he beamed his
pleasure when the Queen enquired about his early adventures with cattle.

Who witnessed more ranchland drama than Billy Henry?
Anyone living at High River for seventy-five years enjoyed the
preferment of a "ringside seat." He was there to see many of
the big herds come in, see the range when barbed wire was
considered an indignity, and ride in the country-wide
roundups with Tom Lynch, George Lane, Dan Riley, John
Ware and other giants of the range.

But the most memorable adventure of his cowboy career
was in taking rawboned Alberta cattle to the Yukon Interior in
1898. Sixty-two years later he seemed to be the only survivor
of those stalwart fellows who delivered beef at Dawson City in
the early years of the goldrush.

> ━ ♦ ━ ◦ ━ ♦ ━ ◄

THE FIRST CATTLE TO THE KLONDIKE were taken over the Chilkoot or White Pass but early in 1898, when the rush was approaching its feverish peak, a new route—longer and somewhat less hazardous—was laid out by Jack Dalton for his pack trains; and Billy Henry, driving cattle for Pat Burns, was one of the first to go over it.

The Scottish immigrant boy was 17 years of age when he arrived by stagecoach at the Highwood Crossing, later known as High River. It was 1885. Buck Smith ran the stopping place and the Macleod Trail, over which I. G. Baker Company bull teams hauled the freight, was the main street. The young Scot, new to a stock saddle, took a job with Spalding Brothers and then with Tom Lynch. In short order he acquired the skills of a seasoned cattleman and began building his own herd. Before long, he was making a bold deal, trading one hundred and seventy-five head of cattle for the High River hotel which had everything a hotel of that period should have—stable, corrals, bar, dining room, eight bedrooms and a well-worn path at the rear. The famous Phil Weinard ran the bar and Henry, still more interested in cattle than in the traveling public, spent most of his time on the range.

Came the news about gold in the Yukon—"nuggets the size of a foal's eye." Calgary's Pat Burns, ever the first to recognize business opportunity, sent cattle with Billy Perdue late in the winter of 1897–'98. These were broken oxen bought in Oregon and selected with special thought to suitability; they could be used to haul or carry their own feed on the trails and be handy in dragging logs for rafts on which their own carcasses would be transported over the last part of the journey to Dawson City. Moreover, the miners were not fastidious about tenderness and wouldn't object to ox meat as long as it tasted like beef.

After being shipped from Seattle, the old oxen with many rings on their horns, were hitched to sleighs and packs at Skagway. Every ox became a beast of burden again and

Perdue took the shortest route over savage Chilkoot Pass and down to Lake Bennett. The ox-drawn sleighs, loaded with feed and supplies, were hauled over the ice as far as the foot of Lake LaBarge where the spring break-up demanded a complete change in mode of travel. There, after the oxen dragged long logs to the river's edge, the animals were slaughtered and their carcasses loaded on the raft to be floated the remaining way to Dawson.

At journey's end, the beef sold as readily as though it were tender, the logs from the raft were sold for building purposes and Billy Perdue and his men celebrated. And when Perdue celebrated, everybody nearby was likely to know about it, as an item of news in the *Calgary Herald* of October 21, 1902, indicated: "A well-known cattleman (Billy Perdue), having remained too long at the bar of the Alberta Hotel, decided to do some fighting. The porter and night clerk overpowered him and escorted him to his room. Soon he loaded his gun and went looking for revenge. Patrons saw a porter and a night clerk racing through the halls and dodging while a cattleman with gun was in pursuit. Constable Fraser got into the act and finally Perdue landed in jail."

>·+·+>·•·O·•·<+·+·<

EVEN BEFORE THE CELEBRATED PERDUE was back from the North, Pat Burns was asking Billy Henry to take a bigger herd to the same remote market. "You cut out a trainload of big steers from my herds on the Little Bow and Mosquito Creek. Make your own arrangements and be on your way."

Henry selected one hundred and seventy-five heavy cattle and loaded at Cayley on a June morning. Strangely enough, the biggest mishap on the entire journey to the uncertain North occurred a few hours after loading. Near Fish Creek the railroad grade, weakened by floods, gave way and sixty-five of the selected cattle were killed in the train wreck.

Superstitious friends were sure it was a warning and Henry should abandon the expedition. But to give up didn't occur to him; instead, he went at once to get replacement stock and in a couple of days he was on his way to Vancouver, escorting one hundred and eighty steers, mostly four-year-olds and five-year-olds, averaging sixteen-hundred pounds.

Duncan Fraser and Bill Summerton, experienced cattlemen, were his chief helpers and at Vancouver he hired six more men. They loaded the cattle and twenty-two horses on a twelve-hundred-ton CPR scow. The livestock occupied pens on the scow and the men had a small cabin. When all was ready, the loaded scow was pulled away at the end of a long cable by a tugboat known as The Mystery.

Pyramid Harbour, where the cattle were landed on the beach, was across the inlet from Skagway and a dismal place. Henry had no desire to remain longer than necessary. Having received advice to try the Dalton Trail—"it'll take you longer but you'll go father on foot that way"—he sought some preliminary directions and on the fourth day after arrival, cattle, horses and men set out over the forest trail leading to the Chilkoot Pass. The first part of the trail, more westerly than the road to the Chilkoot, was level and pleasant with ample feed for cattle and horses. But before going far there was a rude interruption by some well-armed men with the faces of desperados, demanding payment for the use of Jack Dalton's trail.

There didn't seem to be much point in arguing with Dalton's gunmen and the toll was paid. True, it was public property on which they travelled but Dalton's men had cut the trail and the Dalton name seemed to bear some connection with a family of United States outlaws.

>—·◆>—·O—·◆·—·◁

IT WAS NOW THE FIRST OF JULY and the days were long—practically no darkness. If it was scenery men wanted, it was here in abundance and they went over the Chilkoot Pass without mishap. There was an abundance of vegetation in most places but not much of it was grass, and finding suitable grazing was a problem. Bears were plentiful and cattle became nervous, sometimes threatening to stampede. But day after day they plodded on, passed Dezadeash Lake, passed Aishihik Lake, crossed the Nisling and Klaza rivers to reach the Lewes.

Charlie Thebo of Montana, whose name recalled the widely publicized horse drive by Michael Oxarart some fourteen years before, was known to be on the trail ahead but there was no human habitation for hundreds of miles until reaching the Lewes River. Now, following that stream, the herd was driven past Five Fingers Rapids and on to a point close to the mouth of the Pelly River where mountains reached to the water to block further progress on foot.

Autumn nights were becoming increasingly cool and ice was forming on the river. Billy Henry knew there was no time to lose if the last part of the journey were to be made on open river water.

"Go back and find a place to make corrals," he told his men. "We've trailed about five hundred miles and we'll slaughter everything now—float the meat the rest of the way by raft."

In the days that followed the nine men endured long hours constructing corrals, making rafts and butchering everything—horses as well as cattle. A wheel-hoist was devised for raising and handling carcasses and a small sawmill operating nearby was given an order to cut rough timbers—six inches by six inches—for rafts. The cattlemen were as busy as neighbors at a barn-raising.

Each October night was colder than the one before and Subarctic frost penetrated the carcasses and kept them from spoiling. That was exactly as Billy Henry would have it and when the rafts—each seventy-two feet long and thirty-two feet wide—were ready, the frozen carcasses were piled on and covered with a tarpaulin.

Henry figured it was one hundred and fifty miles to Dawson City and when all was ready the loaded rafts with men on board, were released into the river current. They raced over rapids and moved slowly when the stream broadened. Men might have wished for faster current but nothing could be done to change the river's paces and moods.

Correct timing was extremely important. To make this part of the trip earlier would have invited spoiling of the carcasses; and if it were later, the danger of the raft being trapped in ice would be greater. As it was, Thebo, with cattle ahead of Henry's lost meat from spoiling and at least one herd travelling a few days later, was lost when the river froze over.

"We struck it about right," Billy Henry said, "arrived at Dawson toward the end of October." The market was still brisk. The Mounted Police took seventy-five thousand pounds of beef at seventy-five cents a pound while the balance of the beef brought a dollar a pound and the horse-meat sold for dogfeed at fifty cents a pound. All payments were in gold-dust which Henry turned over promptly to the bank at Dawson City to be credited to Mr. Burns.

>−+◆>−◯−<◆+−<

WINTER WAS SETTING IN and when the last of the meat was sold, Billy Henry discharged his helpers and took a stagecoach to the coast. At the beginning of February he was back at Calgary, only to discover that Pat Burns had another shipment of heavy oxen ready to be taken to the North as soon as Henry was willing to leave again.

"This was a different trip altogether," Henry said. "It was a winter trip and we had to take sleighs and feed for the cattle and horses. After landing at Skagway, it took us two weeks to freight our stuff across the White Pass. Then we followed the Dawson City route to a place called Log Cabin and from there had to break trail to Atlin."

Dominic Burns, brother to Pat Burns, accompanied on that trip and at Atlin a Burns butcher shop was opened.

After that the mild-mannered little man went back to ranch life in the South, mainly along the Highwood River, which exerted a special attraction for him.

"What kind of cattle were those you drove to the North?" the Queen asked him. With a whimsical grin, the old timer with a seventy-five-year association with his beloved High River, replied, "Oh, just common critters—but they were as valuable as champions when we got them there."

Moose Jaw to Dawson City

>━┤◆>━O━<◆┤━<

THE TWO TUXFORDS and their brother-in-law, James Thomson, left Moose Jaw on May 24, 1898 with seventy cattle, three saddle horses, and a dog. Five months to the day after waving farewell to neighbors, they were at Dawson City, deep in the chilly Yukon, with the dog and sixty-six carcasses of beef.

One horse died from injury on the trail and the other two were given best wishes and freedom to rustle in the far North. And the discrepancy between seventy steers and sixty-six carcasses of beef was explained by one steer dying from eating poisonous plants, one straying beyond the point of recovery and two having to be shot when their feet "wore out" from walking on rocks and gravel. Yes, their feet "wore out."

The three men were early settlers north of Moose Jaw, close to the village now bearing the Tuxford name. George Stuart Tuxford—later Brigadier General Tuxford, C.B., C.M.G., D.S.O. and bar, organizer and commander of the 5th Battalion C.E.F. in the First Great War—was born in Wales and came to Canada in 1886. In the next year, he homesteaded north of Moose Jaw and was joined by his brother, W. A. Tuxford. And James Thomson who became a brother-in-law, was a veteran of the commonly-called North West Rebellion.

>─┼─◆>─◆─O─◆─<┼─<

WHEN GOLDRUSH FEVER was attacking most able-bodied men, the Tuxfords and Thomson talked about going as prospectors but decided, instead, to follow Ed Fearon's example, stake their chance of fortune on cattle they might succeed in driving to the scene of the mining stampede. Other prairie men like F. O. Sissons of Medicine Hat and Meat Merchants Burchill and Howie of Brandon, were making similar decisions.

The Moose Jaw men bought seventy steers during the winter, selecting mainly cattle rising four years of age and a few broken oxen capable of carrying sizable packs. Horses and cattle for the journey were duly branded and loaded on CPR freight cars at Moose Jaw to be shipped, first of all, to Vancouver.

The freight train carrying the shipment to the coast overtook "five cars of cattle from Brandon, also bound for the Klondike." These were the Burchill and Howie cattle, one hundred four-year-olds bought by W. J. Burchill and being taken to the North under the direction of J. A. Howie. The Manitoba partners had made the wise provision of sending Robert Lane, also of Brandon, on ahead to construct cargo rafts beside the Lewes River.

From the time the Moose Jaw cattle overtook the Brandon stock in British Columbia, the two outfits remained close together on both rails and trails for the balance of the months-long journey.

At Vancouver there was an annoying delay, waiting for the boat *Coquitlam*, on which cattle and all would travel along the mountainous shoreline to the coast of Alaska. The shipment left Vancouver on June 8 and landed at Pyramid Harbour— starting point on the Dalton Trail—six days later.

At once the Dalton Trail became a busy thoroughfare for cattlemen. Several herds were unloaded in the shallow Pacific Ocean water and driven ashore before the Moose Jaw men started over the Trail. Some of the herds were American, some Canadian. Altogether, according to George Tuxford's estimate, two thousand cattle were delivered there for drives over the inhospitable Dalton Trail. Billy Henry with Burns cattle was some days in advance; Burchill and Howie cattle and those belonging to Sissons and Hargreave arrived within a day or two of the Moose Jaw herd and were ready for the trail at about the same time. It was the American, Thebo, however, who had the largest numbers, nearly a thousand head in several herds.

While at the Harbour, cattlemen fraternized amiably and shared information and hints about the ordeals anticipated. But once on the trail, it was every man for himself and Heaven help the person with less than a double portion of resourcefulness.

>—⋯—O—⋯—<

EACH CATTLEMAN HAD HIS OWN IDEAS about driving, planned in most cases before leaving home. In the Tuxford-Thomson scheme, the broken oxen were included specifically for the purpose of carrying packs and hence only three horses were considered necessary, one for each man. Supplies and equipment for the expedition were placed in neat packs of fifty pounds each and two such packages were given every morning to each ox and made secure by means of the diamond hitch.

The cattle walked briskly at first but had to be prodded before reaching the Chilkat summit. Weather was favorable but quickly it became evident that the footing would be bad and the north-country mosquitoes, terrible. There was the added indignity of having to pay toll on Jack Dalton's trail, the only consolation being that other cattlemen were doing the same. The mysterious Mr. Dalton was at that time inaugurating a pack train freight service between Five Fingers Rapids and the Alaskan coast, had two hundred horses assembled for the purpose. But the freighting project was successful for only a brief period because river boats employing cables in surmounting rapids were soon offering a better and cheaper service.

The grazing was generally poor and cattle were obliged to eat willow leaves and twigs as they travelled. The scarcity of grass in that sub-Alpine vegetation increased the chance of trouble from toxic plants. As it was, however, only one steer died from such poison.

At times the cattlemen's biggest worry was the rough river-bottom land over which they were obliged to drive. Sharp rocks and round pebbles cut and bruised even the toughest bovine feet. When cattle became lame, there was nothing to do but stop for a time in the hope of recuperation. Two fine big steers—together worth a thousand dollars at Dawson City—failed to respond to rest. Hooves had become worn down by cruel stones until sensitive feet bled whenever the suffering animals tried to walk. It would be unfortunate to leave such salable beef behind but men realized that delay in a land where winter comes early and viciously could lead to the loss of the whole herd. The ailing animals were shot.

>–·◄›·–O–·‹►·◄

ON AUGUST 12 THEY REACHED THE LEWES RIVER—sixty-six foot-sore cattle, two emaciated saddle horses, three hardy men from Moose Jaw, and the dog. A river crossing was effected at once and the herd then driven a short distance to Rink Rapids. The drive might have continued another fifty miles to the mouth of the Pelly River but forests at Rink Rapids offered big logs for raft construction and the men agreed upon the wisdom of stopping and slaughtering. Moreover, they were becoming more concerned about time; days were shortening, nights were colder, and at that latitude nobody would count on much summer after the middle of August. The fastest way to get to Dawson City with what they had to sell, men agreed, was to begin at once the making of rafts on which to carry carcasses.

There beside the cold water of the Lewes, the Tuxfords and Thomson prepared to set up a meat camp. The immediate tasks were big ones, especially for a small crew of three men. Most of one man's time would be occupied by herding the stock where feed was available, and upon the other two would devolve the tedious work of fashioning rafts and then, in the shortest possible time, dressing sixty-six steers and oxen.

Obviously they needed more help and they could see how time was running out. Up to this point, progress had been satisfactory—at least as good as that of any other cattlemen on the trail—but while men dragged raft logs to the river and tediously dressed one carcass at a time, they saw the herds and rafts of other cattlemen passing. They also saw unclaimed sheep browsing nearby, survivors from a Rink Rapids wreck in which the owner was drowned some weeks earlier.

Billy Henry with Burns' beef was known to be at least a week's travelling distance ahead, and the Moose Jaw men saw most of Thebo's cattle and beef go by on rafts made at Five Fingers. George Tuxford's journal mentioned "Rudion's outfit" running the rapids at Rink with sixty-one cattle on a scow and thirteen on a raft.

Everybody on the trail was now conscious of a great struggle against time. Sissons, having shod his cattle to spare their feet for the drive as far as Selkirk at the mouth of the Pelly, appeared and disappeared. "To vary the stream of stock going down," George Tuxford noted, "two hundred sheep passed in a scow whilst the Burchill and Howie outfit from Brandon loaded in three large scows, also passed down."

It wasn't reassuring for the men from Moose Jaw to see their fellow-cattlemen—in a real sense their competitors—passing them, taking a lead in what was admittedly a race to Dawson City inspired by the advantages of being there before prices sagged under the volume of incoming beef. But they pressed forward with their work, fitting one heavy dry log after another into the construction of two rafts and then converting one big steer after another into carcass beef.

Each finished raft, sixty feet long and twenty-four feet wide, was held together with cross-timbers made secure by stout birch pins. There was no doubt, the rafts were built to withstand the stresses of the most angry water.

➤━◆➤━○━◆➤━◄

AND FINALLY ON OCTOBER 3, all was ready for departure on the last segment of the journey. With moist eyes the men said farewell to the two remaining ponies and turned them loose in the unfriendly northern wilderness. It might have been more considerate to shoot them and thus spare them the suffering likely to accompany the oncoming winter but these horses possessed broncho hardiness and there was a chance they would survive. Promptly the men moved onto the rafts loaded with twenty tons of beef and let the current carry them away.

Now their fate rested with the river; they could go no faster than the current and each night the formations of ice extended farther from the shoreline. Below the mouth of the Pelly they found themselves travelling within sight of the Sissons raft, both outfits in a bitter contest with the Subarctic winter.

The race ended on October 24—exactly five months from Moose Jaw—when the prairie men reached Dawson City. Had they been a day or two later, the river would have been frozen over and the cargoes of beef locked in ice.

With the other outfits reaching Dawson City ahead of them, the local price of beef had dropped considerably but it still looked good to men whose cattle would command not more than three cents a pound back at home. One raft load of Moose Jaw beef—nine thousand, nine hundred ninety-four pounds—sold for 40 cents a pound, less than half of what Billy Henry received earlier in the month.

As soon as sales were completed, the Tuxfords and Thomson began the long journey back to Moose Jaw. Their hope was to be home for Christmas. And like Sissons, they refused to part with the Collie dog which had served so faithfully, even though Dawson City miners, starved for companionship, eagerly bid up to $500 in gold-dust for the animal.

"After being away those seven months taking a bunch of cattle to market," James Thomson said many years later, "Moose Jaw looked awfully good. It looked like a place I never wanted to leave again."

The Trail to Disaster

NORMAN LEE OF THE BRITISH COLUMBIA CHILCOTIN was a good loser. For him the "Trail of '98" was a cattleman's tragedy, returning nothing but costly experience. He lost everything, the beef from one hundred and seventy-five cattle, supplies, equipment and laborious effort.

By the time he arrived back at Vancouver months later, his chattels were reduced to "a blanket, a dog and a dollar." It could be added, however, that he still had his sense of humor and the will to go back to cattle ranching on the inter-mountain grass.

LEE FIRST SET FOOT UPON BRITISH COLUMBIA SOIL in 1882, after making the journey from his native England by way of New York, Salt Lake City, and San Francisco. In the Nicola Valley he learned the art of cow-punching and then worked with crews building the CPR in the mountains. The year 1887 found him in the Chilcotin, west of the Fraser River. In that vast land of grass and trees and scenery, he indulged in trading and started with cattle.

Early in the spring of '98, when talk of Klondike gold was on every tongue, Lee resolved to take his herd of cattle to

Dawson City by an all-Canadian route and on May 17 of that year the great drive began from his place at Hanceville. Two hundred cattle made up the herd and with it were the necessary helpers, five cowboys, a horse wrangler and cook.

Lee divided the herd, allowing each man to drive a small band of thirty or forty head; the cattle travelled better that way, especially in forest country—and for much of the way they would be in forests. At first the drive went forward at ten or twelve miles a day. The cattle were fresh and they might have covered more distance were it not for the fallen timbers blocking many parts of the trail.

Each day's program called for the cattle to start soon after sunrise, leaving the pack horses to move as soon as they were loaded. Spare saddle horses were driven on ahead of the cattle, and the wrangler was expected to stop about noon when he identified good feeding ground. There he would build a fire and prepare lunch for the oncoming cattlemen. After the midday meal, the pack train and cook would move ahead of the cattle to select a suitable campsite for the night. The idea was good but sometimes the man in charge misjudged a normal day's travel for the cattle and made camp too far away.

Along the Blackwater River there were good places to camp but while the cattle were still fresh and keen to return to home pastures, night herding was necessary. A note in Lee's diary, easy to understand, tells that night herding "in pouring rain is the reverse of pleasantness."

Lee was not the only cattleman on the trail; in that diary loaned most graciously by his sister, Miss Grace Lee of Starcross, England, he says, "Of the cattle that started from Chilcotin, Jim Cornell was about a week ahead of us with seventy-five head, Jerry Gravelle about three days with one hundred and we heard that Johnny Harris with two hundred was trying hard to catch us."

Although not acknowledged, there was unmistakable competition between those in charge of the several drives. And the Harris outfit did overtake and pass the Lee cattle.

EARLY IN JUNE THEY WERE ON THE TELEGRAPH TRAIL, about fifty miles from Quesnel. Now, for a limited distance, there was more traffic, "all kinds and varieties of horses, all sorts and conditions of men," all headed northward to the land of easy fortunes.

"At the end of the first day on this trail," wrote Lee, "we camped at Mud River, a small river which seemed to be deep enough to require swimming. An Indian had built a raft and was busily engaged ferrying people, horses and goods across. He must have coined money as his charges were pretty stiff. I made a bargain with him to cross my stuff and then I made a discovery. A little way down stream was a trail leading to the river which I followed and found that I could ford the cattle and pack animals easily which was duly done, and our example was followed by all the other pilgrims who were about to cross with the help of the Indian. The ferryman saw that his business was at an end so climbed into his raft … vanished down the creek."

Lee then made a further discovery, that the ferryman had actually placed a dam on the stream to make the need for his transportation service appear convincing.

The Nechaco River was crossed and at the Hudson's Bay post beside Fraser Lake the cattlemen replenished dwindling supplies. Lee asked the company officer how often he received mail and the reply was, "We never get mail here."

From Fraser Lake to Hazelton the route was largely through heavy timber but it afforded fairly good grazing. A danger to cattle was in poisonous plants; one steer in Lee's herd died as a consequence and Harris lost a dozen or more animals. The treatment for steers suffering from poison, according to local advice, was to "bleed them by chopping off pieces of their tails and feed them with much bacon grease." Evidently the recommendation was not taken seriously.

At Hazelton there was to be a three-day rest stop; the cattle needed it and the cattlemen welcomed it. But there was added delay; Hudson's Bay rum proved to be such an attraction that three more days elapsed before all cowboys were ready for the trail. And to settle accounts with the Bay company officer, a few steers had to be left behind.

Out of Hazelton, they had to swim the Skeena River. Then there was the quaint Indian Village of Kispiox and more rivers as cattle, horses and men moved toward Telegraph Creek.

The Telegraph Trail was gay with native flowers and wildlife, but hazards were increasing. Stinking horse carcasses beside the paths made it clear. Feed problems became increasingly serious; cattle were passing through heavy timber and over mud flats with only occasional swamps offering grass. Horses suffered more than the cattle; according to information furnished by E. D. Sheringham who accompanied Lee on the expedition, the horses became the victims of "mud fever" and began to lose their hooves. In order to spare the weakened animals, all but necessities were discarded from packs, and cowboys even took to herding on foot. But in spite of all the relief offered in this way, the horses became weaker and most of them died on the trail.

>--◆--O--◆--<

BY THE END OF AUGUST, after travelling close to the snow line, picking their precarious way over the summit of Ground Hog Mountain and sometimes skirting dangerous mountain precipices, the cattlemen were some two hundred and sixty miles beyond Hazelton. Worst of all, human food reserves were diminishing all too quickly. Lee walked on ahead to Telegraph Creek and along the way bought flour and bacon wherever possible and "cached it in the woods, blazing a tree with my cow brand so that the boys would know where to find the stuff."

Lee arrived at Telegraph Creek on September 2, a few days ahead of his cattle, and discovered that Jim Cornell who had made good time with his smaller herd, was there and having decided against going beyond that place, was already operating a butcher shop and getting rid of his beef.

To Lee, however, the only plan offering hope of success was to drive to Teslin, there slaughter the cattle and raft the dressed beef over the lake and rivers to Dawson City. A man called McIntosh was sent on to Teslin with instructions to commence building the rafts.

Having forced his cattle across the Stikine River on September 6 and seen them heading toward Teslin, Lee repaired to Glenora to secure another pack train. Three weeks later he overtook his herd, forty miles from Teslin. Then, going on ahead, he rode into Teslin in company with Johnny Harris and Jerry Gravelle and their herds.

McIntosh had the necessary logs ready for scow construction but it remained for Lee to make arrangements for corrals and slaughtering facilities.

Lee's cattle, having completed the first major part of the projected journey, were at Teslin on October 3. Attendants had reason to believe the worst of the undertaking was behind them. The slaughtering began and men moved with an air of triumph.

An experienced butcher hired on the site was able to dress twenty cattle per day while Lee's regular helpers handled another twenty. Hence, the work went forward briskly and slaughter of the last steer coincided precisely with completion of the two scows, each forty feet by sixteen feet in size.

The beef was not all choice, not by any means; the long and hard journey had robbed the animals of any fat they might have had at the start of the trip but Dawson City miners were not fastidious and red meat would be more important than quality.

>-+-<+>-0-<+>-+-<

A FAIR WIND WAS NEEDED to conduct the loaded rafts for one hundred miles across the lake and on the morning of October 17, the breeze seemed perfect. Lee and his men had two days of good sailing but northern weather can be tricky and treacherous. On the third day the wind became strong, then violent. It seemed as though the scows would break. Men attempted to guide them to some sheltered cove along the shore but there was no such haven. Finally, the rafts were heaved against the shoreline rocks. For two days, gales continued and frustrated men were powerless to do more than watch one scow and then the other being wrecked.

The storm ended but what was left for the cattlemen? The beef—much of it submerged—was utterly valueless in that unpopulated part of the North and it was too late in the season to consider the construction of other scows, even if the meat could be salvaged.

There was nothing for it but to accept defeat and abandon the beef. Some of the men accepted Lee's offer of the little boat they brought along and departed toward Dawson City. Lee and Will Copeland said they were returning to Teslin—sixty miles back. Food supplies were divided and men went their different ways.

From Teslin a small party went out to inspect the wrecked cargo of beef and returned with thirty quarters considered possibly fit for food. Of these Lee claimed a percentage but there was practically no local sale for it because of the large number of crippled oxen slaughtered there at the end of the trail. The fact was pretty obvious; the undertaking had ended in complete loss for Lee.

As for the other men who came over the trail with cattle, Harris with a raft of beef was four days ahead of Lee and escaped the fateful storm on the lake but word was received later that his outfit became "frozen in" about two hundred miles above Dawson City and the beef, like Lee's, was a complete loss.

>—+◆>—O—<◆+—<

THERE WAS NOTHING MORE to hold Norman Lee in the North. He and Copeland constructed a hand sleigh on which to carry their few belongings and, with their faithful dog, began the long trek to the coast. Their hope had been to get down the Stikine before it was frozen over but winter came in with a vengeance and the snow was already deep. At Glenora the report was that navigation had ended. So deep was the snow that even the hand sleigh had to be abandoned. Leaving Glenora on December 2, the two men tramped over ice and snow, making their own trail for one hundred miles, and arrived at the Alaskan boundary on Christmas day. After some delay they managed to get across to Wrangel and there catch a boat going south.

It took a stout heart to undertake such a twelve hundred-mile drive through unsettled wilderness and it took a stout heart to accept the loss and return cheerfully to raise more cattle in the Chilcotin. All honor to the memory of Norman Lee.

Honeymoon Behind
the Herd

WHEN CHRIS BARTSCH who became a prominent Alberta rancher made his second trip to the Yukon gold fields in 1900, it was his honeymoon and he was combining business with pleasure by taking along fifty steers and five hundred sheep for the Dawson City meat trade.

"With all that livestock, it wasn't an ordinary honeymoon," the ninety-year-old Bartsch conceded shortly before his death at Calgary in 1959, "but it was a good one and I'd like to do it again—with the same cattle and the same bride."

IN SWITZERLAND WHERE HE WAS BORN IN 1869, the father was a cattle dealer and one of the boy's tasks was to drive Swiss cattle through the valleys of the Alps and into Italy. Thus, when he first saw Skagway, Bartsch was no stranger to either cattle or mountain travel.

At the age of twenty he emigrated to the United States and when news about Yukon gold discovery reached him in August, 1897, he left his job in a Portland, Oregon, packing plant and sailed for the North, eager for adventure and fortune.

At Skagway he saw some of the first cattle arriving. Henry Waechter and Sons brought a hundred head, unloaded them out in the bay and drove through the shallow water to dry ground. The Waechter plan was to hold fifty head at Skagway for the winter but to start the other fifty toward Dawson City as quickly as possible. It was then October and Chris Bartsch accepted the job of taking the advance herd over the winter trail.

With nine helpers and twenty-five saddle and pack horses, he started from Skagway. It required eight days to cover the forty miles over White Pass and down to Lake Bennett—forty miles of mud and snow and rocky inclines. Feed was carried for the horses but the herders depended entirely upon grazing—such as it was—for the cattle. The intention was to construct a scow at Lake Bennett and place the cattle on it but the lake was already frozen and Bartsch was there with fifty steers, winter approaching and no feed.

Plans had been changed. He and his men slaughtered at the lakeshore, froze the beef and waited for sleighs and more horses to be brought from Seattle. The equipment for hauling the meat over the ice didn't arrive until March when weather was beginning to moderate. Nobody could go far on ice after that time of year. But when sleighing failed they salted the meat and built a scow to carry it. Thus Bartsch floated to Dawson and to mark the end of the journey with a well-earned celebration, he treated himself to a restaurant meal for which he was charged $21; revenge came later, however, when he charged the same restaurant operator $75 for a roast of beef. But now, having met with success, the young man decided to remain in the North, set himself up as a Dawson City butcher and commission broker to serve the incoming cattlemen.

>─┤◄►─O─◄►┤─◄

LATE IN 1899, WITH DOUBLE PURPOSE, Chris Bartsch travelled back to Seattle. While negotiating for the purchase of sheep and cattle to be taken north, he stopped briefly to get married and then continued with plans for a combination honeymoon and livestock drive over the most rugged terrain on the continent. What happened after that was best told by the Chicago-born girl, Grace Adeline Graham, who became Mrs. Christian Bartsch.

Leaving Seattle on April 3, 1900, sheep, cattle, and newly-weds travelled in the same boat, *City of Seattle*. There were storms at sea and the livestock suffered as much as the people on board. But at Skagway, Bartsch unloaded five hundred sheep and fifty cattle, exactly the numbers loaded at Seattle. Then, to the flock, he added one female goat bought at Skagway, the thought being that Nanny might prove useful in leading the sheep over difficult trails.

It was his intention to drive all the livestock over White Pass—as he had done before. But with the narrow gauge Yukon and White Pass Railway now operating as far as Bennett, it seemed logical to use it and avoid some of the mountain hazards. Accordingly, the sheep, cattle and horses were placed in thirteen freight cars. While men prepared to travel in the stock cars, Mrs. Bartsch wrapped herself in her husband's fur coat and took a place beside a window of the cramped caboose car. From there she gazed through the night at the snow-covered mountain shapes looming with ghostly indistinctness, while three railroad engines tugged the little train to the summit. She felt unpleasantly alone but reminded herself that there had been honest warning about the hardships awaiting her and it had been her own eager decision to come.

Her introduction to "that queer little place called Bennett" came at two A.M., with the problem of finding a place to sleep where crowded stopping places provided no such luxury as privacy for travelling women.

Bartsch knew he must hurry if he were to travel on the ice. As quickly as possible the outfits started across the lake, four men driving the sheep, two driving cattle, a four-horse team loaded with feed and a two-horse team and sleigh on which Mrs. Bartsch rode. For her, the first day on the ice of long, narrow, mountain-flanked Lake Bennett was fun; even an upset without injury produced a laugh. At night there was a supper of cooked beans, then a tent and bed of blankets spread on spruce boughs—"Klondike feather bed."

On the second day they came to the end of Lake Bennett and because of open water in the stream connecting Lakes Bennett and Tagish, herd, flock, and teams took to the shore line. Tagish offered good sleighing again, and then Lake Marsh. But the ice was becoming more uncertain and horses were increasingly tired. More and more, Mrs. Bartsch found herself walking with her husband, usually behind the sheep.

Open water at the lower end of Marsh Lake invited the construction of a raft to carry feed at least as far as White Horse Rapids. How they would meet the hellhole at White Horse remained to be seen.

Having launched a roughly-constructed raft and started the sheep and cattle overland, Chris and Grace Bartsch accepted an invitation to ride in a little boat with three strangers on their way to Nome, Alaska. It proved to be a pleasant party and they sang lustily as the current carried them along, at least until Chris caught sight in the distance of a man leading two rather familiar-appearing oxen. His first thought was of theft but what he discovered was that one of his steers had gone mad and bolted. A cowboy then took a gentle ox to coax the renegade back. It couldn't be overlooked that every steer became more valuable the nearer it was brought to Dawson City.

>─◄►─○─◄►─◄

THERE WAS LOTS OF ACTIVITY at Miles Canyon and White Horse Rapids—men organizing to portage or bracing themselves to ride through. Bartsch was tempted to let his raft of feed and supplies go with the current but decided instead to pursue the safer course, that of transferring freight to the foot of the rapids by tramway and there constructing another raft. It required ten tramway trips but while making them he witnessed somebody's raft being caught in ice and rocks and "crushed like an eggshell."

Small crosses bearing the inscription, "Victim of White Horse Rapids," made Mrs. Bartsch feel sad but thankful for safety so far. Thinking of home, she robbed a young birch tree of bark and wrote a letter to her mother. "You need not worry about me," she told her, "for Chris with untiring strength, broad shoulders and knowledge of the country, is the kindest and best protector any girl ever had." Then, folding another piece of bark to make an envelope, she sealed it with balsam and saw the outgoing mail taken away by dogteam.

In a few days they were moving again, Chris and Grace Bartsch walking with the sheep. Just after leaving, they had to kill a sick ewe and that hurt because they knew she would have been worth $100 delivered at Dawson. But there was increasing need for hurry; they were determined to cross Lake LaBarge while the ice would still carry herd, flock, and teams.

But LaBarge was a bad experience. It was now May; ice was becoming rotten and, as Chris realized, if they couldn't cross on the ice, they'd have to wait several weeks for open water and that would mean reduced returns at Dawson where only the first drive of the season was assured of a big premium in meat prices.

The raft was abandoned and cattle, sheep, and sleighs started on the thirty-mile trip to the lower end of the lake. Knowing the dangers, Chris was uneasy. The sheep, soon wet and exhausted, moved slowly. At the end of the first day, camp was made at the lake shore and men hoped for a hard frost at night to make the ice firm again. But the night was mild and on the next day, travel was worse. To make matters doubly difficult, mosquitoes came in warlike hordes. "They were so large," according to Mrs. Bartsch, "I felt I could shoot them without being in practice." She sought her veil as a means of protection but discovered that the ever-naughty Nanny goat had eaten most of it.

The sheep sensed danger on the ice and when they came to a soft place near the centre they bunched alarmingly. Ice was sinking and water oozing over it when Chris recognized a crisis and tried to move them. They seemed frozen with fear. Finally he shouted to his wife, "Grace, call Nanny." She called the goat on which she had often lavished affection—"I pet her and tell her my secrets." Nanny responded and the sheep followed, narrowly escaping what in a matter of minutes might have been drowning for all.

"Grace," Chris said, "we've got to get off this ice, even if we never reach Dawson." But by this time it wasn't easy to get off. There was open water close to shore. Only one narrow bridge of ice remained and the sheep were driven over it until it gave way and the last animals fell into the water as they attempted to leap to safety. Chris with lariat was obliged to pull them to land one at a time.

Fortunately, the cattle were making better time but the teams and sleighs were in serious trouble. "Can you handle the sheep?" Chris asked his wife and she replied, "Yes." Taking all the sheepmen with him, he went to help the stranded teamsters while the resourceful bride kept the flock together beside the lake.

Some horses and freight went through the ice that day but Bartsch succeeded in getting his outfit off and then faced the necessity of completing the trip to the lower end of the lake by some devious land route punctuated by snow-filled canyons and wild streams. It was most trying but with perseverance they reached the end of the lake from which point there was assurance of open water all the way to Dawson City.

Bartsch had planned to raft everything from there but the river water was too low to carry heavily loaded scows and the overland journey was extended to Hootalinqua, another thirty miles or so. At that place the livestock were placed on rafts— five of them, each about sixty feet by thirty feet. Two double-decked rafts would carry the sheep, two were for cattle and one for horses and equipment. Loading presented its own problems. One steer jumped the loading chute, landed in the river and swam ashore, to be recovered from the nearby hills with difficulty.

The river's mood changed frequently. Sometimes it was quiet like a lake, sometimes rushing savagely. But even with the necessity of unloading at intervals to let the stock graze and drink, the outfit was now making its best time. The decision was to unload and drive around the rapids at Five Fingers, then "run" the fast water at Rink Rapids.

FINALLY, AT NOON ON MAY 24, the long journey ended at the shack-town where Klondike River met the Lewes. The bride of a few months made herself presentable to face the curious crowd. Cattle and sheep were unloaded—the first to arrive in that year—and slaughter and sale of beef began.

The journey had been long and often dangerous but, Chris Bartsch testified, at no time had his wife uttered a complaint. "I was happy," she admitted, "enjoyed every minute of the wonderful experience." In the following autumn, Chris and Mrs. Bartsch went south for another shipment of cattle and sheep.

But in 1903 they left the Yukon to live in Alberta, work with Pat Burns at Calgary, ranch extensively at Gleichen and enjoy pioneer memories until death took both of them in 1959.

Peddling Bronks on the Winnipeg Trail

>-+>-O-<+-<

WHEN WILLIAM MCLELLAND WAS 14 YEARS OLD and living at Red Deer, his stepfather presented him with horse, saddle, lariat and shotgun and said, "Now young fellow, you're on your own; get out and make your way in the world." That was in 1888.

The youth obeyed, took to the range, rode with some of the best cowboys of that time and drove cattle for Pat Burns when that worthy was furnishing beef to feed the many hungry workers building grade for the new Calgary-Edmonton railroad. Often it was a matter of driving the cattle a hundred miles or more to the slaughter camps but the routine afforded excellent opportunity to learn the skills demanded by the trails. "I could bed down on grass anywhere south of the Red Deer," he said, "and have the feeling of being at home."

It wasn't surprising that along in the '90s, McLelland was starting away from the Bow River with four hundred horses— destination: Winnipeg. The trail of his choosing would be one of more than a thousand miles. "Might sell some horses along the trail if we go by the North," he was saying, "and what we don't peddle on the way, we should be able to sell in Winnipeg."

The McLellands were Michigan people who settled where the Calgary-Edmonton Trail crossed the Red Deer River. The boy was ten years of age when they went to that place to farm

and operate a stopping place made distinctive by the only shin-
gled roof between Edmonton and Calgary.

⋗━╍⋗╍⊙╍⋖╍━⋖

A YEAR AFTER THEY SETTLED BESIDE THE RIVER, they heard
war drums. There was fear of the Duck Lake trouble spreading
and the McLellands saw troops marching northward on their
trail; they saw Montreal soldiers building a stockade around
their stopping place and converting it into a fort. And among
those who lined up to receive an issue of guns was the eleven-
year-old boy who had already learned to chew tobacco and handle a muzzle-loader with the best of men in the home-guard.

One of his first jobs for wages was as assistant to the skinner of an I. G. Baker Company bull-train. The outfit operating
between Calgary and Fort Macleod had forty-eight baleful
"bulls," driven in three units of sixteen each. And the wrangler
in charge possessed qualities scarcely more refined than those
of his oxen. Not only did he "cuss" his work cattle throughout
the daylight hours on the trail, but he talked in his sleep and
"cussed them all night too."

The same skinner had a parson as passenger on one trip to
the South when the big wagon outfit bogged in mud. Out of
respect for his ecclesiastical company, the driver exercised
unprecedented restraint in language. It was all very well to omit
such words as the clergyman would find offensive or beyond his
understanding but there was one obvious trouble; the oxen
weren't impressed by mild language and showed no inclination
to extricate the wagon. It was perfectly clear to anybody who
understood oxen and drivers; some more drastic action was necessary if long delay in the mud was to be avoided.

In desperation the vitriolic man of the wagon-trail turned
to the reverend gentleman, saying, "Parson, either you stick
your fingers in your ears for a few minutes or we'll be in this …
mud-hole all night."

Accepting the hint, the minister stopped his hearing and the
bull-whacker went into one of his oft-repeated addresses to the

oxen. Now the animals understood and as they responded by pushing vigorously against the yokes, the heavy wagons moved slowly from the mire to firm ground.

But Bill McLelland was more interested in horses than in oxen and was gaining recognition as a skillful handler. The trouble was that horses on the western ranges were becoming too numerous and the incentive to breed was vanishing. After the severe winter of 1886–'87 in which cattle suffered more than horses, many ranchers turned to breeding what they considered the hardier animals. It was reasonable to expect that settlers flocking to homestead lands would be eager to buy horses, any horses. The homesteaders, however, had some bad experiences with bronchos wanting to run away or kick the seed drill to splinters, and favored the eastern stock.

><+>•O•<+><

BY 1894 THE HORSE MARKET was really depressed and growing numbers on the range were doubtful assets. It was at this point that Bill McLelland resolved to gamble on a big drive through homestead country and into Manitoba. He had some horses of his own and it was easy enough to get more, either by purchase at prices as low as $5 a head or rounding up unbranded broncho stock to which nobody bothered to lay claim.

With three friends game to undertake the all-summer expedition with him, he gathered four-hundred head and herded them northward. Carrying a minimum of camping equipment tied to saddles, men and horses swam the Red Deer near the Crossing and veered northeasterly to pass Buffalo Lake. The country was open, there being practically no settlement until they were east of where Wainwright was located later. Near Battleford, trade in horses began to improve. More settlers needed power and most of them couldn't afford to be very particular about what they chose to pull their walking plows. When a homesteader came out to buy horses, McLelland's price was $15 per head, the buyer to take his choice. Nothing in the entire band was broken beyond resentful familiarity with a halter, so there wasn't much choice.

To facilitate finding the horses when they strayed, the men took to placing bells about the necks of some. The result was more far-reaching than anticipated; it was soon observed that when settlers bought horses from the big herd, they invariably chose the ones wearing bells, supposing, no doubt, that such animals had been handled.

Resourcefulness being a horseman's trait, McLelland and his helpers began belling the poorest horses and found as they travelled and made sales, the average quality of remaining horses was improving. Upon reaching Winnipeg, they had none but the best horses and CPR buyers looking for horses to work on grades were greatly impressed.

There were many unusual experiences along the route. How could such a trip produce less? Halting for a day of needed rest in the Qu'Appelle Valley, the travellers found themselves under constant observation by Indians on a nearby hill. At first there was fear of a plot to steal horses but then the real reason became evident. Nearby was a "tree burial." A year earlier, two medical students had gone through this part and pilfered an Indian corpse for purpose of anatomical study. The Natives were incensed and taking no chance of a repetition, even though the Indian agent assured them that horsemen would be totally disinterested in dead bodies.

Even more touching was the encounter with a family of American land-seekers, completely stranded where the four mules upon which they depended to haul their covered wagon, had strayed. It was uninhabited country somewhere between Battleford and Saskatoon. The mules had departed during the night; possibly they had been stolen by Indians but, anyway, two weeks had elapsed since their disappearance, making it seem unlikely that the lost animals would ever be located. More than that, the family food reserves were running low and parents were desperately anxious about the safety of their children. Already they had killed most of the hens being taken to the homestead they envisioned and were facing the necessity of killing their milk cow.

Never did stranded people have greater need for a good Samaritan and in this instance they found four of the kind. A piece of bacon, fifty pounds of flour and four bronchos were turned over to the ill-fated land-seekers. The men from Bow River helped to break the wild things to harness and then went on their way, wondering how the prospective homesteader from Missouri succeeded in mastering the bronks, speculating if the undomesticated horses would prove to be a blessing or a curse.

>─┤◆├─○─┤◆├─◁

NOT LONG AFTER THIS ENCOUNTER, McLelland lost his entire band of horses—about three hundred head at the time. It was not the practice to corral or herd the horses at night. Usually the animals would graze peacefully and settle near where the day's drive ended. The men would hobble their saddle mounts and make their own beds on the Prairie. Then, in the morning, the band was nearly always within view and after a hasty breakfast and a rough count to confirm that nothing was missing, the drive was resumed.

But on a morning which found them somewhere east of Saskatoon, the men awakened to see only their hobbled saddle horses. Nobody was alarmed, it being easy to conclude that the horses had merely grazed their way beyond a knoll or some poplar bluffs and would be retrieved quickly. But gathering the horses for the day's drive was not that easy. They were nowhere to be found and only with difficulty were the men able to pick up the tracks and establish the direction of their departure.

With growing uneasiness the men galloped in that direction—southward. Nobody was overlooking the possibility of theft, perhaps the scheme of rustlers who had been following for days, awaiting an opportunity to strike and whisk the band away toward the International Boundary. If this were the work of professional rustlers, they would be well armed and ready to fight for possession of the herd. But McLelland and his three companions rode on stubbornly, hour after hour, more than ever convinced that their horses were moving under human guidance. Finally, a settler whose place they passed confirmed the fears; he had seen the band being driven to the South—at a fast pace.

After riding hard for most of two days, McLelland and his men came upon their horses, unexpectedly, many of them showing signs of exhaustion. Beyond any remaining doubt, they had been driven hard by rustlers. But where were the thieves? Had they become alarmed as they came into settled country or were they merely hiding somewhere while the horses rested for the next lap in the desperate drive?

In any case, McLelland and his men were not waiting around to learn the answer. In the shortest possible time they collected the tired and stiffened stock and pressed eastward. At the first opportunity, the mystery was brought to the attention of the Mounted Police. And at night thereafter, one of the men rode herd on the band but the culprits were never actually seen.

The drive continued without other major interruption. Around Indian Head, Virden, and Brandon there was brisk demand, homesteaders buying horses about as fast as McLelland's cowboys could tie bells on them.

WHEN THEY FINALLY DROVE into the City of Winnipeg—two and one-half months after departure from Calgary with four hundred head in the herd—the McLelland crew was down to thirty horses. They were the best of four hundred—the ones which had never been belled—and they sold readily to railroad contractors at the inspiring price of $100 each.

The tall, spare, resourceful Bill McLelland bought a new hat for each of his cowboys and a big supply of chewing tobacco for himself. It had been a one thousand two hundred-mile trip the way they travelled, he figured. "But it was a good trip," he insisted, "and if it wasn't so late in the summer, I'd do it again."

"Uncle" Tony and the
Turkey Track

"UNCLE" TONY DAY, REMEMBERED WITH AFFECTION around Medicine Hat, had the double distinction of driving the biggest herd of cattle into Western Canada and, five years later, taking the biggest winter losses in the country's history.

The most vivid local memories were of a full-faced, jovial little man riding a stock saddle as though some degree of adhesion was indicated. Almost as familiar was the mental picture of the same famous cattleman—partially crippled from a hip-fracture in latter years—hobbling down Sixth Avenue at "The Hat" and entering the Cypress Club. There he would slump in the big leather-covered chair to which he, as past president of the executive club, had a special claim.

IT WASN'T THAT A. J. "TONY" DAY was one to seek special privileges or exclusive surroundings. On the contrary, this man born in Texas in 1849, figured half of the food consumed in his lifetime was taken at the rear end of a chuckwagon, and he'd spent as many nights on ground sheets as in beds.

The important fact was that Tony Day, whose experience with cattle extended from the Gulf of Mexico right through to the Canadian grass, was considered by many observers to be one of the greatest stockmen of his generation—on either side of the International Boundary. Best of all, it was a brand of greatness which lessened in no way his modesty and friendliness and willingness to share the stories of his past.

The Cypress Club offered no more enticing fare than Tony Day's tales. Once ensconced in the blubber-fat chair, the stage was set for reminiscing—back to the Rio Grande where he spent early years and on the trails fanning out from that well-favored range. Sure he could ride, rope, and shoot before he could write, and his memory was reliable.

"What about that buffalo you put your rope on one time, Tony?" somebody might ask to more or less "prime the pump."

"Oh sure, sir, a buffalo critter on the end of a lariat can give a feller plenty to think about. It's not like snaring an old cow to get some milk for your coffee. But every young lad has to do some fool things. I figured I was pretty smart with a rope and I had a secret hankering to catch one of those wild devils. Well sir, I rode out of the river brakes one day, not athinking of anything especially, and there, right in front of me was one of those humped-back bulls, aswitching his tail sort of mean like and not sure which way he'd run.

"Perhaps I wasn't playing very smart but I wanted to satisfy myself I could snare that fellow, and my bay pony was game for a run. A buffalo critter isn't slow, you know, but I had a good bit of horseflesh between my legs and we closed in enough for me to get my loop on that bull's horns, neat as anything you ever saw. Now don't ever think the buffalo wasn't surprised—and mad as hell. For a few minutes he was just exploding in all directions and then there was a regular tug-of-war between him and my pony but the bull had the weight and we were being dragged in the general direction of Montana.

"By now," Tony continued, "I was kinda seeing where I'd made a fool mistake. I had a bull by the horns, just as I aimed to have; but what in thunder was I going to do with him. I coulda let him go but not without losing my good lariat. Couldn't afford to lose that rope and didn't want to shoot the bull because by this time there weren't many of his kind left.

"You wanta know how I handed that situation? I'll tell you. You see I learned to shoot about the time I was weaned and I whipped out my six-shooter—we'd no more go riding without our guns than we'd go without boots and chapps—and my first shot cut the rope just behind the honda. Just lost three inches of my good rope."

>-+◆>-•-O-◆>+-<

NOR DID ANYBODY KNOW MORE ABOUT TRAIL HISTORY than Tony Day, and the Cypress Club, hung with trophies of the chase, heard about wild stampedes in the dead of night, shooting war with rustlers, hilarious cowboy sprees marking the Kansas ends of long drives, and Indians sniping at cattlemen as they drove northward. On one of those trail trips a bullet from a sniper hiding in the rim-rock killed the horse Tony was riding. Presumably it was an Indian who fired but nobody among the cowboys ever did see him. And nobody was inquisitive enough to go searching for him.

There were seven boys in the Day family. All who were old enough carried arms in the Confederacy army and all became cattlemen of distinction. Before Tony was born, the father was herding Texas Longhorns into Missouri and after the Civil War, all the Days joined to harvest the semi-wild cattle on those good ranges close to the Gulf of Mexico.

In 1869, Tony's brother, William—known widely as Colonel Day—drove fourteen hundred cattle to Abilene, Kansas, and shipped from there to Chicago. Tony, twenty years of age, made his first long drive at that time and next year rode out with three thousand of the same brother's cattle, headed for Leavenworth, Kansas. But in the latter year, the Days arrived at trail's end to find the market glutted and prices failing. Financial loss faced them but they were resourceful people and, instead of selling at prices which would have meant sacrifice, they slaughtered and packed the beef in salt and shipped it to New York where the result was a handsome profit.

Immediately after the Civil War, Tony Day, still in his teens, assembled a herd of Texas cattle and marked every critter with his own brand. For five dollars a head a man could buy longhorn cows and if he didn't have that amount of capital, he could gather unclaimed stock which had eluded both the men with branding irons and those gathering herds for the trail to Abilene or Dodge City.

Rounding up unclaimed Texas cattle was legitimate at that time or Tony Day wouldn't have been doing it. The man who became so well known as a Canadian rancher believed in branding his own cattle and his own only. "Pay the duty on cattle you bring in," he told his fellow Americans settling in Canada. "Pay your taxes and pay your debts."

>—I—◆>—O—<◆—I—<

ABOUT 1875, TONY AND A BROTHER became attracted by grass in the more northerly states and drove their herds to Nebraska. Cattle numbers grew rapidly until they had twelve thousand head. That was fine until the memorable winter of 1886–87 when cattle losses were so high that Tony Day, like many other cattlemen, was almost out of business. He returned to the Panhandle and there entered into partnership with Henry Cresswell. Again the herd expanded under good management and Cresswell and Day needed more grass. Again they looked to the North and in 1895, Tony Day was directing four thousand head to the Black Hills of South Dakota, where the partners supposed there would be no competition for grass.

By the beginning of the new century, Cresswell and Day cattle in South Dakota stood at an imposing twenty thousand head and again there was the haunting feeling of settlers pressing in on the range, robbing cattlemen of their security.

"Where else is there to go?" Tony asked and the answer: "No place unless you cross the line into Canada."

On the Canadian side at that time, the foothills and Prairies contiguous to them were fully stocked but there was still a big expanse of less popular prairie range bordering on the Cypress Hills. Tony Day set out to reconnoitre—on a sturdy Turkey Track pony, of course—and there south of Swift Current, south of Maple Creek and south of Medicine Hat he found grass in sufficient abundance to support his huge herds. He had never considered running cattle so far from his native Texas but the grass was there and it looked attractive.

In the summer of 1902, the Turkey Track cattle were in motion again, twenty-four thousand head of them, and six hundred horses, moving still farther north and west. It was the last of the major cattle shifts and it may have been the biggest one. The route led out of South Dakota to Billings, Montana, and then north to cross the boundary at a point due south of Maple Creek.

Dust rose in clouds when the several herds totalling twenty-four thousand Turkey Tracks, grazing as they travelled, inched their way north and into the Northwest Territories. Little Tony—five feet, six inches tall—like a general riding from one battalion to another, gave guidance to his lieutenants, carried information about waterholes in the country ahead, and tried to make peace with the settlers who saw the transient cattle eating all the local grass and drinking up the last traces of water in their sloughs.

At the border, Day paid $40,000 to meet the duty demands of the Canadian Customs and at once the cattle population of the Northwest Territories increased sharply. The Turkey Track was now a Canadian brand and Tony Day, whether he realized it or not, was making the last of his many long drives.

>─◆◆─○─◆◆─◇

THE CANADIAN GRASS WAS GOOD ENOUGH to inspire an observant rancher, and the men of the northern range were friendly. But the Canadian winters were holding some heartbreaking surprises and reverses for the Turkey Track. First there was the May storm of 1903, just a few months after the herd arrived in

the Territories. Cows were calving and the young cattle were
scattered. Spring days were misleadingly lovely and then came
the unexpected return of winter. For three days the snow came
in on a savage gale and cattle drifted. Weakened by hunger and
exposure, many perished. Turkey Track losses were said to total
two thousand cattle of all ages.

That May storm was a cruel baptism for immigrant stock
but when the results were compared with Turkey Track
deaths in the winter of five years later, they seemed small
indeed. "Terrible" was the word men used to describe the
conditions of 1906–07 when snow was deep, frost unrelent-
ing, and storms frequent. Cattlemen with small herds and
piles of prairie wool managed reasonably well but nobody
with stock wintering outside escaped some degree of hardship and loss. On the plains, cattle losses ranged from twenty
to forty percent and springtime brought disgusting displays
of bloated and rotting carcasses in coulees and fence corners
and along railroad tracks. And Tony Day who did everything
in a big way, lost in similar proportion. Turkey Track losses
were estimated at ten thousand cattle, including six hundred
herd bulls. It was enough to bring any but the richest ranching companies to ruin.

In the summer before, Mrs. Day said, "Tony, you've an
awful lot of debts." Her husband's reply was, "Yes, but I've an
awful lot of cattle." Came spring and Tony Day still had the
debts, with fewer cattle.

⋗⋅⋅⋄⋅⋅○⋅⋅⋄⋅⋅⋖

FINANCIALLY IT WAS A BITTER TEST but Tony Day managed to
continue—until, with settlers crowding in on him again, he sold
his cattle and then his horses. In 1916 he was accepting retire-
ment and more time for his memories and his friends and the
Cypress Club.

The injury which left him lame came with a fall from a
horse. When hospitalized at "The Hat," his room received so
many flowers from loyal friends that the old rancher contracted

hay fever but the blooms expressed a good deal of the feeling Alberta people held for Uncle Tony Day, who chose to terminate his long cattle trails with them.

"A Horseman Called Bowlen"

►─┼─◄►──O──◄►─┼─◄

JACK BOWLEN, WHO BECAME ALBERTA'S sixth Lieutenant-Governor, trailed horses from points in Southern Alberta to Humboldt and Macklin in Saskatchewan so many times that, according to his telling, farm dogs along the way quit barking at him.

"I'd rather trail horses than wait for a freight," the man of action said, "and often there was no freight to where I wanted to go anyway."

Southern Alberta had cheap horses; Saskatchewan had settlers needing them and as J. J. Bowlen discovered, the most economical transportation over the six hundred miles from point of surplus to point of need was under their own power. "I could leave Macleod or Calgary with thin horses in my bunch and have them in pretty good flesh by the time I reached Saskatoon or Humboldt," he said. "Usually lost a few pounds of my own weight but that didn't matter."

►─┼─◄►──O──◄►─┼─◄

STRANGE, BUT THIS MAN who so completely mastered the long distances represented by his horse trails, grew up in Prince Edward Island where great distances were unknown. If he distinguished himself in anything on The Island, it was at milking cows and picking potatoes. But the will to travel burned in his youthful heart and when he heard about jobs paying good wages in Boston, he borrowed $15 and went to that city which seemed to be full of Nova Scotians and Islanders. In his first job he was a teamster, in the next a street car conductor collecting $2.25 for every twelve-hour day. Then there was a stint of army service in the Spanish American War and he returned to Prince Edward Island with a wife and a thousand dollars in savings.

In 1900, the twenty-four-year-old "Spud Islander" journeyed to the far Northwest where he worked for $15 a month, rented a Manitoba farm, and then bought a quarter section near Muenster, Northwest Territories. There followed a series of difficult years, due mainly to frozen crops. But the enterprising young man remained busy, cutting and selling firewood, feeding frozen wheat to pigs, and trading in horses.

The horse business held a special attraction and the opportunities were apparent. Every homesteader wanted more horses as soon as he could pay for them and to aggravate the existing shortage, swamp fever took a disastrous toll in that area. Bowlen's horse deals were becoming more numerous and in 1909 there was the first of his major trail journeys. A brother who went to Southern Alberta wired to have him investigate a certain business opportunity at Nelson, British Columbia. On the return there was a stopover at Macleod. Restlessly, Bowlen sat in the hotel lobby, putting in time until the hour of train departure.

The train was late; "trains were always late in those days." While he waited, with no lessening of impatience, a band of one hundred and fifty horses was driven along the street in front of the hotel. Horses could arouse Jack Bowlen's interest at any time and in an instant he was on his feet, instinctively following toward the stockyard where the animals were being penned. There they were, bronchos, driven in from the West. Yes, they were for sale—$55 per head. For one hundred and fifty head that would be $8250. He wished he had that much because he was sure he could sell such a band at Humboldt or Muenster.

The train Jack Bowlen had been waiting to board came in and left without him. His mind was temporarily on other things and before he turned away he offered the owner of the herd $50 a head—$7500 for the lot. Perhaps, at that late autumn season, Bowlen shouldn't have been buying horses but he wanted these. And for better or for worse, the owner accepted the offer. Excitedly, Bowlen wrote a cheque for the full amount, forgetting that he didn't have that much in either cash or credit.

The unpleasant consequences of reckless cheque writing soon dawned upon him and he communicated at once with his banker in Humboldt. To his surprise and relief, he heard that the cheque would be honored. Now, what was to be done with the horses? It would be folly to take them to Humboldt at the onset of winter. They'd sell better in the spring and he arranged to run them for the winter in a strawpile field at High River where his brother was in the implement business. At once the horses were driven toward that place and a man hired to watch them until spring.

AS SOON AS SNOW HAD MELTED IN 1909, Jack Bowlen was back at High River, making arrangements for the long drive overland—six hundred miles at least. He bought a chuckwagon, hired three riders and a cook, and gave the signal to start.

Nobody in the party had ever been over the proposed trail route and a railroad map was the only guide. The map showed villages and towns but neither roadways nor rivers. Marked was the Village of Brooks about due east of High River and the cook was instructed to drive thence. "We'll swing north from there," Bowlen offered; "probably hit the Red Deer River but we've got to cross it somewhere."

The men drove hard for the first day so horses would be tired and easier to hold at night. It was planned that one of the riders would remain on guard at night but even at that it would be less difficult if the horses were sufficiently fatigued to make them forget the urge to return to more familiar surroundings.

An old grey mare in the band wanted to turn back from the minute of departure and was seen as a potential trouble maker. But the first day and first night passed without incident more delaying than that of pulling a couple of horses out of a boggy water hole. "What's more helpless than a horse in the mud?"

On the fourth day they forded the Bow River and stopped a few miles short of Brooks. "Tomorrow morning," the boss announced, "we make an early start and get by that place before the town people are out of bed. There'll be no buggies and wagons on the roads and we can push right through. Maybe make it to the Red Deer tomorrow night."

Carrying out the plan, the horsemen saw the prairie town when only a few early-risers were about. There was no need to stop but the men little realized that in appearing and disappearing so rapidly, they were inviting suspicion and a police investigation.

If the outfit reached the Red Deer by nightfall, there'd be assurance of water and the men would consider the best way of crossing. Unexpectedly, they came to water in the afternoon and learned that the stream from which the horses drank was Ware Creek. Sure enough they were crossing the range of the late Negro rancher, John Ware, killed right there in a fall with his horse, three years earlier. Bowlen had never met Ware but knew of his great skill as a stockman, knew of his strength and the affection with which he was held by everybody around him. The ranch, at this time, was being operated by Rod Macleay, who became one of the giants in the industry.

>─┤◆>─○─<◆├─<

YES, EVENING FOUND THE TRAIL MEN in the badlands beside the Red Deer. And frightening was the sight of the river—swollen to several times its normal size by flood waters and frothing madly in its new-found might. It was a terrifying sight to say the least. What was to be done? A squatter beside the river confirmed that there was no bridge either upstream or down and added, disturbingly, "Be two or three weeks before the water goes down much."

Jack Bowlen, to be sure, wasn't sitting there for two or three weeks, waiting for water to subside. "I don't like it," he told his men, "but if we're going to swim it, let's do it now. Why wait for morning? The wagon can go up or down and maybe find a ferry but we're going to hit that water right now. Come on boys."

There was still the delicate matter of persuading the horses to take the plunge. They'd allow themselves to be driven to the water's edge and then fearfully veer away. The squatter settler and another came to help and the attempt to rush the horses into the flood was repeated. Finally, the old grey mare took the lead in stepping timidly into the water. Other horses followed and in an instant they were swimming and fighting the current carrying them down stream. The horsemen knew they must follow and once at swimming depth, with horses facing the opposite shore, each rider slid from saddle, into the water, and seized his mount's tail as an aid in swimming.

Men knew the flooded river held danger but this was worse than expected. Whirlpools tried to draw men and horses under and floating logs introduced added hazards. A horse disappeared and then another. How many more would be sucked to drowning deaths? The impetuous decision to cross was seen as a mistake but it was too late to change anything and horses and men continued the life-and-death struggle with the current.

There was a feeling of hope when the grey mare climbed out upon the farther shore and genuine relief when all the men were again on dry ground. They had been carried almost half a mile with the current and there were losses—nine horses drowned—but thankfulness filled the men's hearts. There on the north side they prepared to spend the night without chuckwagon and without blankets. But the men were happy to be alive.

WHAT THE HORSEMEN DIDN'T KNOW while struggling in the river, they were being pursued by officers of the law. At a Mounted Police Veterans' reunion at Calgary many years later, an ex-Mountie was recalling some early assignments in pursuing horse thieves. There had been a lot of stealing and a gang of rustlers was known to be operating near the "Bar U" Ranch. When a band of horses was driven through Brooks at an unusual hour, "travelling pretty fast," Constable Whiteoak was instructed to follow.

Overtaking wasn't easy, however, and the constable arrived at the river just in time to see the horses emerging on the other side. To follow in that swollen, swirling stream seemed like suicide and the officer chose to telegraph ahead and have some other member of the force intercept the travellers. That was done and the reply was, "A horseman called Bowlen on his way to Humboldt. No horse thief."

Almost at once Jack Bowlen encountered an Indian with spare horses and bought enough to make good the drowning losses. Now he was on his way again, driving across unsettled country with water holes too far apart for comfort. After days of travel, the village which came into view was Provost and for much of the remaining way, Bowlen had railroad right-of-way to guide him. Increasingly, there was evidence of settlement, and homesteaders came to bid on horses. Sales were made at Macklin where the Bowlens were to make their home for a time, at Unity, Wilkie, and Biggar.

At Saskatoon, the herd crossed the South Saskatchewan River on a new traffic bridge and was driven over ground on which the first University of Saskatchewan buildings were under construction. And after nearly two months on the trail—two months of sleeping on the Prairie—Jack Bowlen arrived at Muenster with over a hundred horses, the others having been sold along the way. There in the Humboldt area the demand was strong and sales were made quickly, giving the horseman a profit of roughly $10,000. Nothing more was needed to make the undertaking a satisfaction and Jack Bowlen went back to Southern Alberta for more horses. Thereafter, a drive was an annual event until he became an active Alberta rancher, raising horses and cattle and sheep on his various places.

>—◄►—◦—◄►—◄

OF COURSE HE HAD OTHER INTERESTS, including politics which took him to the Alberta Legislature. And as Alberta's Lieutenant-Governor for almost ten years prior to his death late in 1959—at age eighty-three—he was still the horseman and cattleman at heart and still the man to whom thousands of westerners, with affection in their voices, referred to as "J.J." or "Jack."

The Big Pig Drive
to Gleichen

GEORGE THOMAS "HOG" JONES who raised pigs by the thousands in his Southern Alberta community of Arrowwood, had other claims to distinction, among them his fabulous pig drive of 1915. The Canadian farming country witnessed nothing to rival it. One can readily understand the amazement of a stranger from a nearby town who watched the extremely slow approach of widely scattered men on foot and what seemed like a shapeless wave of dark bodies moving silently, almost mysteriously, through the prairie grass.

Nobody at the time considered the news value or the unusual significance of the drive. To neighborly spectators, George Jones was simply taking a year's crop of pigs to Gleichen where the uninspiring animals would be loaded on freight cars and sent to Chicago. Friends who joined to help the undertaking were too busy to see much romance in it.

MOST PEOPLE HAVE HAD STRONG VIEWS ABOUT PIGS— rarely endearing. Generally, those who have faced the necessity at some time of driving them—into a stable, down the road or out of the garden—can explain convincingly why the race was once considered the abode of the Devil. Prejudiced cattlemen have been known to argue that even Satan deserved a better habitation.

In trying human patience through the ages, no domestic animals have rivaled pigs. And the Jones drive, numbering five hundred of those self-willed creatures across miles of prairie country could reasonably be expected to compound the ordinary range of conflict between people and pigs.

Human guidance has always been hateful to swine, something to inspire a defiant plunge in the direction of forbidden things. Bulldozer tactics made popular by earth movers and football players were adopted with a minimum of change from the inherent ways of pigs.

Because they possessed neither the flocking instincts of sheep nor the responsiveness of cattle and horses, it is not surprising that pigs, in the years of primitive transportation, were accorded the privilege of riding in wagons, carts and canoes.

The first pigs at Red River Settlement—two bought from the North West Company post on the Assiniboine in 1814—were delivered by canoe. A short time later, seven pigs were being brought from England for the new Experimental Farm. It was mid-winter and the pigs were wrapped in buffalo robes to prevent freezing and tied down to sleds on which they were being transported across the ice. One may well imagine the piggish protests breaking the winter silence on Lake Winnipeg.

As everybody should know, some of the most stirring chapters in North American history involved drives of cattle, horses and sheep but rarely did anybody consider the trailing of pigs unless there was no alternative. Consequently, exceptions were the more noteworthy.

At least one heroic attempt was made to take one hundred and seventy pigs from Skagway over the Chilkoot Pass, to Dawson City in the years of the gold rush but there is nothing to show how the owner, Elkjor by name, got along on the trail of ice and snow.

Fortunately, there are those who remember the Jones pig drive of 1915, saw it at the onset and saw it at the finish. It took three and one-half days and covered about twenty-five miles—not far compared with some of the great cattle drives—but nevertheless a huge undertaking, involving as it did almost a quarter of a million pounds of pork on the hoof.

Jones, six feet, two inches tall and weighing two hundred and twenty pounds, was born in Tennessee and raised in Missouri. In March, 1909, he brought his family to Alberta and settled on a three-quarter section farm about twenty or twenty-five miles south of Gleichen. Hundreds of Missourians were coming with settlers' effects, attracted by cheap land and fertile soil. George Jones, like the rest of them, intended to grow wheat, perhaps on a large scale.

But Jones would be a conspicuous fellow in any group. He was a natural leader. Being strongly religious, he started non-denominational church services in his Arrowwood district. His obvious luxury was tobacco—in any form; when he wasn't chewing it he was smoking it in pipe or cigar. Neighbors said he would burn out an ordinary pipe in three weeks.

>━┥◆〉━○━〈◆┝━<

YHE YEARS 1909 AND 1910 WERE DRY and wheat yields were low in that part, about seven bushels per acre. The next year, 1911, was different but no more rewarding. Rains were adequate and the Red Fife wheat, growing rank and heavy, matured more slowly than usual, becoming the victim of an early fall frost. It was a difficult crop to harvest. Much of it lodged and binders were able to operate only one way in the fields. Worst of all, the grain was so damaged that the crop was scarcely worth cutting and threshing.

The first load of threshed wheat hauled over the long road to Gleichen brought forty cents a bushel and drew a pronouncement from the grain buyer that he would take no more like it. Jones, needing money and being unable to sell his wheat, was understandably worried. He had eight pigs on the farm, not nearly enough to eat the unsaleable grain. He wished he had eight hundred and immediately resolved to raise more—many more.

In the spring of 1914, the pig herd reached fifteen hundred head, mostly the red Duroc Jerseys and black Poland Chinas. At the same time, the Jones cattle herd had grown to two hundred and fifty head and horses to one hundred—about all he was able to graze on the Blackfoot Indian Reservation. Now his intention was to have enough pigs to eat all the grain grown on the farm, by this time three sections in extent.

Jones raised pigs in Missouri, even herded them to market on occasions there. It was natural that he would bring many of the American farmer's ideas about pig breeding with him. He saw no reason for hurrying a pig to market weight; better, he figured, to let it grow slowly and economically, rustling much of its living. Consequently, the spring of 1915 found him with over five hundred yearling pigs on the farm, about three hundred and fifty pounds on the average, and ready for introduction to self-feeding and fattening for market. The hoppers on the Jones self-feeders were taking close to three tons of ground grain every day that summer and the Durocs and Poland Chinas ate and grew fat. The pig yards radiated contentment.

>─┤◄>─●─<►┤─◄

ALONG ABOUT MIDSUMMER, a Chicago man—Shansey by name—came that way. He had land interests in the Arrowwood district and he sometimes bought livestock for shipment to Chicago. Never before had he seen so many fat pigs on one farm and he wanted to buy them. Jones admitted that he was ready to sell if he received what he believed the pigs to be worth. "Make me an offer," he suggested.

The man from Chicago counted the pigs, studied them, estimated weights, did endless arithmetical calculations and said assertively, "I'll give you $25,000 for them; you could smoke good cigars for the rest of your life with that kind of money."

But Jones was no novice in estimating weights and said, "No thanks, until you can offer me $30,000 you're wasting your time and mine."

There was a counter of offer of $26,000, then $27,000 and $28,000. Jones said, "You're getting closer but too low yet."

"All right," replied the Chicago man, "I'll make you one more offer and, so help me, it's my last. I'll give you $28,000 and a new Ford car and you deliver the pigs as far as Gleichen so they're all shipped out at one time."

"A new Ford car and $28,000," Jones repeated slowly. "A new Ford and $28,000. All right, it's a deal. We'll load the pigs at Gleichen. Don't know how we'll get them there but we'll manage it somehow."

Yes, Gleichen was nearly twenty-five miles away and there was no such thing as a farm truck for hauling pigs. Jones decided to take the porkers to the railway siding on their own feet, do it slowly and hope the weather would be favorable. There would be no short-cuts. Saddle horses would be of little help in driving pigs and even the farm dog would be of limited use. Men on foot were what was needed and quite a few of them.

>·─·◆·─·O·─·◆·─·◁

AT SUNRISE ON THE DAY APPOINTED, five hundred fat pigs averaging about four hundred and fifty pounds were released from their feed yards while George Jones, five sons and four other helpers began turning them toward the north. For half an hour there was sheer pandemonium with fat pigs spurting madly in all directions. The men seemed utterly useless until the novelty of release from pens ended and, becoming tired of their own disorder, the pigs accepted the trail to the north as the course offering the least opposition. Pedestrian herders urged the animals on and following closely behind the drivers were two horse-drawn wagons loaded with grain for the pigs and bedding and food for the men.

There wasn't much problem in finding water for the stock because the first part of the journey was along East Arrowwood Creek to its mouth on the Bow River, thence along the river to the bridge, and finally across the Indian

Reservation toward Gleichen. Crossing the Reserve could have presented water problems but Jones knew how to zig-zag his course in order to strike water holes, including Susie Lake. Fortunately, the days were not excessively hot or the drive might have been in trouble; fat pigs are readily susceptible to heat prostration. As for feed, grain from the wagons was simply placed on the ground three times a day and the pigs recovered most of it.

Nightfall of the first day found men and pigs only five miles from the starting point. There was no corral but none was needed. Pigs were tired and ready to bed down on the prairie grass. Men felt and did the same.

On the second day there was somewhat more progress as measured in miles—about eight miles—and the chief difficulty was at the Bow River bridge where the pigs balked in the best pig fashion. But Jones, anticipating everything, had provided frame panel gates which were set up at the approach to the bridge and after some assorted arguments with pigs choosing to bolt toward home, the herd was on the structure and testing its strength.

On the third day, Blackfoot Indians gathered to watch this strange parade. Silently they let it pass. The drive was nearing an end. At sundown pigs and men lay down within sight of the town and next day the teamsters went ahead to see that the whitewashed stockyards beside the railway track were ready for the reception of the big herd.

＞─┤◆＞─○─◁＜┤─◁

THE PIGS WERE PENNED SUCCESSFULLY. In the course of the four-day campaign there had been no losses and no mishaps. Stockcars were spotted, pigs were loaded at about sixty-five per car, and the consignment billed to Chicago. George Jones accompanied the shipment and sons and helpers turned toward home.

It will not rate in glamor with the early cattle drives. But somebody estimated that a twenty-five mile drive with a big herd of pigs must be comparable in grief and annoyance with a five hundred mile drive with cattle. Be that as it may, the Jones drive was a gigantic undertaking, one more of the triumphs in a period when human resourcefulness was necessary.

Eppard's Unparalleled Sheep Drive

DRIFTING SOIL FILLED THE SASKATCHEWAN AIR and depression filled men's hearts in that spring of 1933 when Sheep Farmer Marion Eppard decided to move—quit the farm beside the Souris River in the southeast corner of the province and hope to keep his flock.

From Estevan, Saskatchewan to Vernon in the Okanagan Valley of British Columbia may be less than a thousand miles as the proverbial crow would fly but for Eppard and his wife and five-year-old Kenneth taking a year and a half to drive the sheep over a tortuous and at times terrifying route, it was a good deal longer.

"We just did it a day at a time," said Mrs. Eppard who was born and raised in Saskatchewan, "and it didn't hurt us." But in spite of such modest assessment of the adventure, it must rank among the most difficult and remarkable sheep drives in history.

TRYING TO MAKE A LIVING beside the Souris River during the '30s was grim for all concerned. Sheep found little upon which to graze except for Russian thistles, notorious as a cause of scouring. Moreover, it took better than an average seventy-five pound lamb to bring $3.50. But instead of liquidating the sheep flock, exchanging the last means of livelihood for a few dollars of cash, Iowa-born Eppard with the fortitude of Dutch ancestors, resolved to abandon the Saskatchewan farm and move the sheep to some more favorable location. Where that better location offering grass instead of Russian thistles might be, he had no idea. "Maybe somewhere west."

Anyway, right after shearing in the spring of 1933, Eppard loaded a few belongings on a farm wagon provided with home-made box, hitched the team, rounded up the three hundred sheep with the help of his Border Collie dog and headed toward the West. Total cash assets at that moment were $3.40. Mrs. Eppard drove the team and wagon, and Marion Eppard drove the sheep.

Not knowing where he was going, there was no reason to hurry. Sheep are never in a hurry anyway. Grazing as they travelled, the animals advanced between four and six miles a day. At each nightfall the band was ready to settle down without the necessity of being corralled. The Eppards pulled a canvas over the riding pole of the wagon and made their bed on the floor of the box.

Food for the family consisted largely of mutton but when more was needed, Eppard slaughtered an extra lamb and traded meat for sugar, tea, flour, and salt. Family requirements were few and simple.

Although they had no known objective, the course for the balance of the summer was roughly parallel with the International Boundary and not far from it. The months passed and the onset of cold weather at the beginning of November found them in Southern Alberta, south of Foremost. Paul Medhurst and his neighbor were threshing in the Goddard district when Eppard came that way. Said Medhurst, "He sure looked the picture of poverty—no clothes for that winter weather. I gave him my sheepskin coat and when I found he had a wife and youngster in the wagon, I gave him a box of groceries from our cook-car."

The next man Eppard met was Joe Determan, a couple of miles to the west, and with pity in his heart, Determan pointed to an abandoned shack on the Charlie Swanson homestead and said, "You better stop for the winter. I'll give you a stack of straw for your sheep."

Gladly the Saskatchewan people accepted. In spare time, Marion Eppard did work for neighbor Jim Hollihan and took milk and feed in payment. When he needed more groceries, he drove thirty-five miles to Milk River, contending that he could get more for his limited money there than at nearer stores. And during the winter, son Kenneth started to school at King's Lake.

>—•◇•◇—<

CAME SPRING AND EPPARD WAS RESTLESS to be pursuing the search for grass. As early as possible he sheared his sheep and hauled the wool to Lethbridge—seventy miles—by team and wagon. Then the Eppards were on their way again. With lambs they now had six hundred sheep.

They passed Warner, then Magrath, and came to Pincher Creek. By this time their money from the sale of wool at four cents a pound was exhausted and they were again getting groceries and other necessities by barter. They traded mutton for a second sheepdog and then acquired a milk goat the same way. "That goat was wonderful," Mrs. Eppard declared. "With a gallon of milk a day, we sure lived good." And the goat was to prove helpful in other ways.

The course was taking them into the Crow's Nest Pass where sheep were something of a novelty. Adults and children congregated to watch as the flock went through Blairmore, then Coleman, Fernie and Cranbrook. Mountains were closing in on them and they should have been worried about the trail coming to a dead end. From Cranbrook they might have continued to follow the road to Creston and around the south of Kootenay Lake but the sheep were getting sore feet and to have softer footing, the flock was turned toward Marysville and then along the St. Mary River which rises in the snow-capped Selkirk Mountains.

People who came out from Kimerley to see the wonders of a band of sheep told Eppard he was a fool if he thought he could take the flock over Rose's Pass to the other side of the Selkirk Range. "Why," said one resident, "there's only a poor footpath and it would be hard enough to make your way over if you were walking alone. And, golly, that's grizzly bear country you know."

But Eppard was a man of determination and he now had exactly two choices: turn back or try to go over the top. He wasn't turning back. The flock was driven forward on the north side of the river and Mrs. Eppard was breathing words of thanks for the goat: "at least we'll have milk and meat." The trail became thinner. The deadfall trees presented more obstacles, some of them having to be cut and moved; the 9000-foot Mount Evans seemed to hang over them like a threatening monster, rock slides rumbled close to them and sure enough, the bears were there.

Just as people had warned, the St. Mary River had to be crossed and re-crossed. But Eppard refused to be frightened. At one point he had to make a bridge by dropping big trees across the gorge; then there was the struggle to get the sheep to cross after the goat was led over in advance. When it became impossible to go farther with the wagon, the heroic people packed personal belongings on the backs of their two horses and pressed on. Eppard would go ahead, choosing a route and clearing deadfall. Then, when the horses could go no farther, they were left behind on the mountain-side, the Eppards continuing on with their sheep at the rate of a mere mile or so a day.

FINALLY THEY REACHED THE SUMMIT and concluded that the trip down the west slope to Kootenay Lake would be easier. At this point, Eppard left wife and boy to continue without him while he walked back, hoping to find the horses. It wasn't easy but he located them, led them to where the wagon had been abandoned, hitched and drove south to Creston, from which point he followed a route along the west side of the mountain range.

The western slope was not as steep as the eastern, and Mrs. Eppard found the fourteen mile decent with altitude drop of

more than 4400 feet to be less difficult than the climb. One of
the problems was in finding feed for six hundred sheep in those
mountain forests but "nothing died from starvation." Only one
ewe was lost in going over the Selkirks, that one having been
severely snagged. But even that was not a total loss because the
ewe was dressed and the carcass taken along for use by family
and dogs.

A. R. McGregor was scaling logs on Crawford Creek when
he heard the bleating from higher up on the Pass and wondered
if he was dreaming. "It sounded like sheep," he said, but it
couldn't be: "impossible that domestic sheep would be coming
over these mountains."

And Eppard, after being lost a few times, drove north along
the lake road to find his wife and boy waiting for him and wondering how he'd cope with the next obstacle—the long and
deep Kootenay Lake lying across their path. An appeal for a
scow sent to a government office at Nelson brought reply that
the service would cost $50. Not having that much money,
Eppard looked for some other solution. He walked to Riondel,
met somebody who knew George DeMille who had a float with
small motor on it. Yes, DeMille would help a man in trouble;
he'd loan his raft.

Eppard built a railing around the flimsy structure and
found he could load fifty or sixty sheep at a time. Fred Watts
of Riondel offered to be navigator. Happily the lake was calm
at the time although smoke from forest fires hung low over
the water and visibility was poor. But with good fortune
through two and a half days of operations the entire flock was
delivered at Mile Point, a short distance south of Ainsworth.
Eppard paid his benevolent friends with the only settlement
possible, three sheep and some small change to pay for the
gasoline used.

THE TRAIL LED TO KASLO, thence to New Denver and Nakusp,
then southward along Lower Arrow Lake to cross by ferry to

Needles. There was nothing in that forest and rock-bound country to cheer a sheepman. But now Eppard was thinking about the Okanagan Valley. He had never seen it but what he heard was inviting. He drove over the Monashee Mountains on a trail built in part by German prisoners from the First Great War.

The season was now well advanced and there was snow on the Monashee Pass. But by this time the Eppards had lost all sense of fear. They drove on and on until the soft scenery of the Okanagan became a reality. About Lavington, between Vernon and Lumby, a pioneer sheepman, R. A. Davidson, met up with the sheep—between five hundred and six hundred he believed—and enquired of the sheep herder where he was going.

"Don't know," Eppard replied. "Do you know any good place to run sheep?"

Astonished, Davidson learned that the drive started in eastern Saskatchewan and mercifully suggested that the travellers use his fenced pasture nearby until they could make better arrangements. The offer was accepted and with the pasture went the loan of an old and long-deserted house on the property. Sitting on an apple box, the only thing resembling a piece of furniture, the courageous lady heaved a sigh and said, "It's certainly nice to be sitting in a real house."

At Ellison, not far south of Vernon, the prairie people were granted permission to winter their sheep in a big orchard. It was journey's end, at least temporarily.

Neighbors who knew something of the British Columbia topography could scarcely believe the story of the long trek, that these people from Saskatchewan, total strangers to the mountains, had followed the only course by which they could have come through at all. And the lad, not very robust when the trip began, was now a healthy specimen and a full year and a half older.

Becoming established with a big band of sheep in the Okanagan Valley was neither easy nor simple but, one way or another, the resourceful Eppards succeeded, finally buying a place fifteen miles north of Kelowna, on the west side of the lake. There they remained until Marion Eppard's death in 1942.

MANY AND STRANGE were the fruits of prairie depression and drought in the '30s. One of the most amazing was the Eppard sheep drive from near Estevan, across hundreds of miles of prairies, mountains and forests, arriving at journey's end with a flock which was not only in good condition but had doubled its size. Where in any land was there a sheep drive to compare with it?

Other Drives—Bees,
Bears and Bulls

THERE IS FRAGMENTARY INFORMATION about other drives bearing the unmistakable marks of ingenuity and daring—enough to make students of Western Canadian story regret the inadequacy of pioneer records.

If fable has intruded in the telling of certain driving escapades, there need be no surprise. How could it be excluded and why should it be? A modicum of fantasy has its place. Those who want only the truth will have no difficulty in separating the facts from the fiction. Readers may treat as they choose, the early Manitoba story or legend about the Selkirk Settler who loved honey and "herded" a swarm of bees from Minnesota to Fort Garry. Nobody is asked to believe it yet, surely, a country's story would be very much the poorer without those touches of romance.

IN THE FOOTHILLS ONE MAY HEAR ABOUT the "Bar U" cowboy who encountered a couple of brown bears when driving a group of herd bulls from Macleod. The urge to shoot and win two good bear skins burned fiercely within him but being without a gun, some other course was necessary; he herded the wild animals in with the bulls and drove all together for the next two days. Arriving at the ranch headquarters, he simply borrowed a rifle and without ceremony dispatched his bears.

Perhaps the story, like that of the bees, has been embroidered with the telling. But scarcely less novel was the authenticated drive of turkeys from the Pacific coast, over chilly Chilkoot Pass and on toward Dawson City at the time of the Yukon gold rush. Where the owner gathered the turkeys is not known. Nor is it known how far he succeeded in travelling with his unwilling and noisy flock but a note in the Kamloops Sentinel on November 8, 1898, indicates success at least as far as Lake Bennett. Joseph Cannel, formerly of Kamloops, had just returned from Dawson City and reported meeting the man going inland with eight hundred turkeys as he passed through Bennett.

It is regrettable that more is not known about Ed "Wildhorse" Johnson's drive of mustangs in 1888. This robust son of Old England who went to South America, broke horses for the government of Chile, and worked his way overland through Peru and Mexico to the Western States and British Columbia. There in the new province he rode for the Douglas Lake Cattle Company. In 1882 he drove one hundred horses through the Crow's Nest Pass to Fort Macleod but still bigger and tougher tasks lay ahead. What must now appear as the nigh-impossible assignment came from Thomas Bean of Alberta's Stud Ranch in 1888 and Johnson and Charlie Perry agreed to go into the Big Bar Mountains of British Columbia to gather wild horses and drive them to Alberta.

Five hundred of the semi-native, unbranded, equine outlaws of all ages were corralled and herded out. To be sure, they were about as rebellious as any captured wild creatures fighting for freedom would be. No doubt the full story was an exceedingly rich one, as completely packed with action as anything concocted for western movies.

>—I—<>—O—<>—I—<

TO RETURN TO CATTLE—some of the weirdest drives on Canadian or United States soil were no doubt conducted by rustlers who played for big stakes. They were drives conducted in a hurry, disregarding all the rules of herd management. One of them, holding special interest for Canadians, was made in 1894—a drive of nearly three hundred miles with river crossings at the Oldman, Highwood, Bow and Red Deer Rivers.

The Cochrane Ranch south of the Oldman was losing cattle, mostly big steers, three-year-olds and four-year-olds. The police were notified but clues were completely missing until an unidentified herd of three hundred or four hundred heavy cattle was seen travelling north about midsummer.

Sergeant Arthur Brookes was detailed to investigate and succeeded in tracing the mysterious herd as far as Olds with some difficulty. There he discovered startling evidence. At the Burns Ranch, only a few miles east of Olds, he was attracted by some recently-acquired steers, bought only a few weeks earlier from a transient cowboy and branded very clearly with a big O.

Careful examination confirmed the policeman's suspicions; the "O" brand had been made by changing the Cochrane "C" with a running iron. It was the handiwork of an expert. A hundred head had been purchased by the Burns agent and the balance of the mysterious steer herd driven on north, destination undisclosed.

The police officer continued his pursuit and discovered where other steers wearing the big "O" brand were sold to farmers along the trail. The scent of stolen property was becoming ever more pungent and the mounty was drawn to and beyond Wetaskiwin. Finally, the evidence brought him to the homestead of a man who had worked seasonally on south-country roundups and was familiar with the Cochrane Ranch and all the surrounding terrain with its coulees offering hide-away shelter for a rustler's corrals.

But at the farm on which the officer expected to question the suspect and perhaps make an arrest, there was nobody home. A few unsold steers with the "O" brand were left behind but the culprit had taken flight. From what was learned, the sharp homesteader, dressed in the expansive clothing of an aged Indian woman and mounted on a decrepit pony, had ridden south over the main trail through Red Deer, Calgary, and Fort Macleod just a few days before. Without arousing fresh suspicions, he crossed the

International Boundary and, according to stories told in ranching circles in later years, became a successful United States cattleman.

Nobody will extol the crime of cattle stealing but at least this operator qualified to number among the notable and successful drives of herds on Canadian trails.

>⊶⊷⊙⊶⊷<

IN ASSESSING CATTLE DRIVES, distance should be fully as convincing as numbers in the herds. Though the big Cochrane herd of 1881 captured most public attention, a comparatively small herd—two hundred and eight cattle—owned by A. P. Patrick and driven the eight hundred miles from Winnipeg to Calgary at precisely the same time should rate about equal recognition. The trouble is that not much is known about it apart from scattered references left by Patrick and a brief paragraph in L. V. Kelly's book entitled *The Range Men*.

Patrick, a government surveyor who pioneered in the search for oil in Alberta, was among the first to recognize opportunity in the foothills and prairie grass. In 1881, after three years in the West, he bought the cattle near Galt, Ontario, and shipped them to Winnipeg—as far as anybody could ship by rail at that time. From Winnipeg the cattle were driven by Patrick and two assistants, Sandy McDonald and Jack Ellis. Leaving Winnipeg on April 10, they reached destination west of Calgary in early fall. Presumably they were five months on the trail and at its end the cattle formed the herd foundation on the Mount Royal Ranch beside the Ghost River. Sad indeed that a more complete account of the drive cannot be presented.

Nor are long drives of livestock on western trails entirely a thing of the past. In the thinking of most readers, those extended overland journeys with cattle or other livestock will be associated with the early years, and quite correctly; but even in this age of accelerated transportation—fast freights, supercontinentals and ranch-to-market cattleliners—a few stockmen make annual drives of considerable size and consequence.

In the year 1948, when the American market was reopened to Canadian cattle, shipping became almost impossible because of a general shortage of freight cars. It was then that Alberta witnessed a brief revival of old time trailing. Self reliant men with an affinity for stock saddles demonstrated that they could still do it when necessity demanded.

After Montana interests bought one thousand cattle in the vicinity of Medicine Hat, Canadian cowboys with a well-stocked chuckwagon trailed the herd south, halted long enough at the George Ross ranch on Milk River to permit the necessary veterinary inspections and then continued on to cross the border at Coutts and head toward Chester, Montana.

The same 1948 circumstances of freight car shortage led Jack Morris and four others to take seven hundred horses by trail from Youngstown, Alberta to Swift Current, Saskatchewan—a fourteen-day trip which included the necessity of swimming the South Saskatchewan River north of Swift Current, in the best old time fashion.

There are still a few annual drives made with the same regularity as the coming of tax notices. In June of each year, two thousand or more sheep belonging to Edwin Davidson of Coaldale, Alberta, are shipped by rail to Coleman in the Crow's Nest Pass and from there are herded for three or four days along the Kananaskis road to summer range on Vicary Creek in Alberta's Rocky Mountain Forest Reserve. In the fall the same trek is made in reverse.

>—◇—○—◇—◇—<

FINALLY, THERE ARE THE CHILCOTIN DRIVES, the longest beef drives still being conducted annually on the North American continent. Originating somewhere far west in British Columbia's Interior and terminating in most cases at Williams Lake on the Pacific Great Eastern Railway, the drives vary greatly in size. Sometimes riders start only a dozen head and arrive at the railroad with two hundred comprising stock added by ranch operators along the route.

Between Williams Lake and the coastal range of mountains is a vast and rugged country, sparsely populated and unknown to most Canadians. Much of it offers grazing for cattle. As there is no railroad nearer than Williams Lake, there is but one practical way of getting the cattle out—drive them. And so, depending upon whose cattle are on their way to market, the trip may be one of seventy miles and take a week, or two hundred and fifty miles and occupy a month.

If they are the Anahim Lake or Tatla Lake cattle, or from the far country of which Rich Hobson wrote in "Grass Beyond The Mountains," they will experience all the tests and dangers presented by the trails of seventy-five years ago. There'll be bridgeless rivers to cross, roads blocked by fallen trees, high passes topped with snow, swarms of blood-sucking blackflies, meals at the rear end of a chuckwagon, and beds on the ground.

There'll be none of the old dangers of surprise attack from hostile Indians but there will be the constant possibility of a stampede triggered by the appearance of a bear or the antics of a bull moose. And one of the new hazards along the trail will be the sudden appearance of curious tourists with fancy clothes and expensive cameras. The cattle from far Anahim Lake take saddle horses and mounted men for granted but humans on foot can strike such terror to their bovine hearts that they will want to stampede to the opposite side of the nearest mountain.

>─┼─◄►─◦─◄►─┼─◄

IT MUST BE EVIDENT that a lot of important history was made on the trails over which cattle, horses, sheep, and other livestock were driven in pioneer and more recent years. And though Canadians have been slow about telling their part of the great story, what took place on the dusty trails leading into and out of this country was in no way less admirable or less exciting than what occurred on the Chisholm Trail or the Goodnight Trail.

Canadian stockmen have their traditions—rich ones.